PRAISE FOR
WINNING THE MONEY GAME

"I recommend *Winning the Money Game* to any NBA player, athlete, entertainer, or young professional. It is a great guide and should be used as a tool for success." —J. J. Redick

"*Winning the Money Game* is a one-of-a-kind must-read. Adonal has lived the life and writes from his vantage point as a thirteen-year NBA vet." —Pat Williams, senior vice president and cofounder of the Orlando Magic

"*Winning the Money Game* would have been great to have back when I was playing for the Harlem Globetrotters, helping me avoid some costly mistakes. Foyle tells it as it is." —Roy Byrd, former Harlem Globetrotter

"Every athlete should read *Winning the Money Game*. In fact, every person should read this book. It's a road map to avoiding financial disaster, combining financial sense with common sense, that shows athletes how not to go from riches to rags." —Ron Barr, host of *Sports Byline USA*

"Adonal Foyle was instrumental in helping me become financially confident. This book will empower athletes like me to go into retirement secure in our financial future." —Marcin Gortat, center for the Washington Wizards

"The long, sad history of penniless boxing champs has become all too common in the NBA. Adonal Foyle's book *Winning the Money Game* is a must-read for every professional athlete. This book is replete with important advice for everyone determined to enjoy over his lifetime the financial benefits of a successful career."

—Neil Grabois, dean of the Milano School of International Affairs, Management and Urban Policy, The New School

"As a nonathlete, I didn't understand sports contracts, nor did I understand the monetary abuse which caused players to go into bankruptcy. *Winning the Money Game* not only explained this paradox, but additionally some of the contents made me call my accountant. This book reaches across aisles with lessons most of our parents and education systems failed to teach."

—Dirk-Thomas Brown, small business owner

"*Winning the Money Game* should be a mandatory read. Foyle makes the learning process enjoyable, easy to understand, and uncomplicated, making retirement planning a true priority for anyone."   —Drew M. Moomaw, CFP® and CEO

"*Winning the Money Game* is an entertaining and informative practical guide for any player, coach, teacher, student, mentor, counselor, or anyone who has a chance to impact young people. It is a story of our times. It is a story of entitlement that must be addressed if we are going to point the 'Me Generation' in the right direction."

—Brian Billick, Super Bowl–winning head coach

"I have the utmost respect for Adonal, dating back to my freshman year at Syracuse when we played together. *Winning the Money Game* can undoubtedly change the lives and guide the paths of many for decades to come. Adonal lays out a concise plan that will keep future generations of sportsmen from falling into some of the pitfalls and mistakes that end in tragedy. Much respect to Adonal for this invaluable guide."

—Etan Thomas, former NBA player, writer, and poet

"Adonal Foyle provides insight into the lives of young men and the sociological pressures that lead to an astounding statistic: over 50 percent of NBA players are destitute within five years of retirement. *Winning the Money Game* serves to attack the root causes of this systemic problem. Foyle is attempting to reach young people early in life, to offer them tools so that they can pursue their dreams."   —Byron Williams, national columnist

"As a licensed clinical therapist who treats the issues that arise from the complex career and family dynamics experienced by those in the sports entertainment and celebrity industries, I found *Winning the Money Game* to be not only inspiring but unique, in that it offers valuable clues on how to preempt or address many financial problems."   —Carla Lundblade, MS, LPC, NCC

"Many professionals—particularly those who enjoy an extended period of lofty income—eventually find themselves without enough capital to support themselves. A critical component to protecting a financial legacy is mitigating risk. This takes on an expanded meaning for professional athletes. Foyle has done a thorough job of identifying the inherent risks associated with men and women who possess such fortunes."

—Ahmed Stephens, financial consultant

WINNING
THE
MONEY GAME

Amistad

An Imprint of HarperCollins*Publishers*

WINNING

THE

MONEY GAME

LESSONS LEARNED FROM THE FINANCIAL FOULS OF PRO ATHLETES

ADONAL FOYLE

FOREWORD BY
J. J. REDICK

HarperCollins books may be purchased for educational, business, or sales promotional use. For information, please e-mail the Special Markets Department at SPsales@harpercollins.com.

Originally published in a different form as *Why Players Go Broke* in 2012 by AFE, LLC.

FIRST EDITION

Designed by Suet Yee Chong

Library of Congress Cataloging-in-Publication Data has been applied for.

ISBN: 978-0-06-234260-7

15 16 17 18 19 OV/RRD 10 9 8 7 6 5 4 3 2 1

To my mother, Patricia Foyle, and to my stepparents, Joan and Jay Mandle. In a world where many people do not have parents, I have three wonderful people who care for me greatly.

CONTENTS

FOREWORD

I believe that things happen for a reason and that meeting Adonal Foyle was not a coincidence. After seven seasons in the NBA and playing alongside dozens of teammates, I can say with confidence that Adonal is one of the most well-rounded individuals I have met. As teammates from 2007 to 2010, we spent countless hours sitting together on the team plane and having dinner on the road.

One of the ways Adonal Foyle stood out was his willingness (and eagerness) to become a student and learn. Just as he was a student of the game of basketball, he also became a student of his finances. Our talks about money sparked my own interest in improving my financial literacy and guaranteeing that I was doing everything I could to secure my future.

Adonal is in the position of authority and expertise to write *Winning the Money Game* because he has handled his money the right way. I have personally witnessed him making weekly financial plans, preparing his taxes months before they were due, securing himself for a successful life after basketball. Because of Adonal, I believe that taking control of my finances is not a choice or a luxury—it is a responsibility.

My time as an NBA athlete will one day come to an end, and I will be fiscally prepared.

It is a sad fact that over 50 percent of NBA players are broke within five years of retirement. Part of the problem is that we are not doing a good enough job of educating ourselves on finances. *Winning the Money Game* not only explains why professional athletes go broke but also provides practical tips and examples of how NOT to go broke. Throughout the book, the examples of Steady John and Big Baller Tom paint a perfect picture of what pitfalls to avoid and what steps to take to save and protect your money.

Winning the Money Game is a wonderfully detailed book about the monetary circumstances of NBA players. Almost none of us come from wealthy families. The vast majority of us do not even come from middle-class families. Instead, we sign multimillion-dollar contracts as twenty-year-olds with little or no financial knowledge. While all of us would admit that we are blessed, at times it is a tough road to navigate. With the help of this book, I believe we can navigate that road with more success and ensure success in our post-NBA lives.

I am fortunate that Adonal is my friend and mentor. I have sought him out for advice numerous times. While not all of us can have a personal relationship with him, this book is full of his wisdom and experience. I would recommend *Winning the Money Game* to any NBA player, athlete, entertainer, or young professional. It is a great guide and should be used as a tool for success!

—*J. J. Redick, guard, Los Angeles Clippers*

INTRODUCTION

We roll up to the club in a Bentley. All eyes are on us as we stroll toward the door in our Tom Ford suits. We know we're going to get comped at the door. We play for the Orlando Magic and they comp us every time. Of course, in the minds of my teammates being comped at the door means more money to spend at the bar! But that's not how I play it. I don't believe in wasting money, period.

As an NBA player, it is easy to get wrapped up in a lavish lifestyle. When we go to the airport, people carry our bags. We travel on chartered planes to various locations where strangers offer us handouts. At restaurants, everyone wants to buy us a meal. Women throw themselves at us, some of them willing to do anything just to be close to us. Admittedly, the lifestyle can become intoxicating.

NBA players live a life of fame and full-out fortune. Well-known and recognizable on the street, the average basketball player earns $5.15 million per year. It's no wonder these twentysomethings are all over the club scene, hotels, strip clubs, and anywhere else women congregate. It's a nonstop party.

I played in the NBA for thirteen years, and over those years I saw extravagances that you would believe a movie director dreamed up, from "makin' it rain" thousands at a time, to pouring Moët on naked women. It's all part of an athlete's lifestyle.

Most players live in mansions—large mansions. If you were to pop over to visit LeBron James, you would enter a 30,000-square-foot mansion near his hometown of Akron. He has a sports bar inside his house. He has an aquarium and a barbershop. He also has an online casino in case you're feeling lucky. The master bedroom suite includes a two-story walk-in closet. I can't imagine the amount of clothes it'd take to fill that up.

It is standard fare for an athlete—and other entertainers—to have pools, saunas, and even guesthouses. Many players take it to a whole other level with luxuries such as large fish tanks built into the wall or expansive recreational areas with pool tables and bars. They have a garage that can hold ten cars. They have a banquet-size dining room, an indoor basketball court, a bowling alley, and, for some, even a football field.

With a home like this, why would you ever leave? For a vacation, of course. Traveling and spending on lavish vacations are not foreign to athletes. Players travel extensively during the off-season, visiting exotic islands with their girlfriends or wives. With the entire summer off, players have considerable time to come up with new adventures.

Custom cars are pretty common with players around the league, too. Classic Impalas, custom Benzes, and brand-new

Bentleys are all cars you see in the player parking lot at any practice facility.

In short, players create a dream life. It seems that they have it all. LeBron is not the only pro athlete with an aquarium. Dare I say they're fairly common? Kobe Bryant amped it up by having a shark tank inside his California mansion. He also has the standard swimming pool, spa, outdoor kitchen, and fire pit. Step inside and you'll find an 850-square-foot home gym, a home theater, and, of all things, a hair salon.

This is a lifestyle we see on television and in movies. Aside from the superrich or the people we've been referring to lately as the "One Percent," this lifestyle is out of reach— even for guys making an NBA salary. Players often stretch the money they earn too far by purchasing big homes and fancy cars when that money, earned over a few short years, is supposed to last a lifetime. An $8 million contract is not enough money for you to buy a $4 million home, but no one ever explains this to young guys in a way that gets through to them.

Most athletes don't make the kind of money LeBron and Kobe pull in, but attempt to live as though they do. Buying a million-dollar home means paying taxes on that million-dollar home. It means maintaining that million-dollar home, including repairs, housekeeping, and utility bills. Is there a pool? Pool maintenance is not cheap. Nor, I would imagine, is the upkeep of a hair salon!

When regular Joes become superrich overnight, whether they're rookie athletes or Powerball winners, most of the time they don't know how to handle the money and within a few short years end up broke or, worse, in debt. This happens simply because they didn't have a plan to maintain their money before they got it. Most just have a plan on how to spend it. Starting in childhood, everyone has daydreamed about what he or she would do with a million dollars. We have countless ideas when it comes to creative ways to spend money, and people who started with little or none often try to put all of their dreams into play at once.

Mike Tyson famously kept two white Bengal tigers in his Las Vegas mansion. The animals cost him a cool $70,000 apiece, not to mention the $4,000 per month he had to drop for food and trainers.

Chad "Ochocinco" Johnson, a former standout wide receiver for the Cincinnati Bengals and later the New England Patriots, had a custom aquarium headboard fit onto the bed in his mansion in Florida. Now, he can literally sleep with the fishes. How much does a fish tank headboard run? It was reported that Chad's cost $11,500.

Athletes may look the part, but in actuality, they are not rich enough to enjoy these lavish lifestyles. Study after study shows that most professional athletes go broke within a few years of retirement. But you don't need a study when you can see it for yourself.

Mike Tyson *did* file for bankruptcy after owning those tigers, but they weren't the only reason he went broke. Iron Mike has made all kinds of questionable purchases throughout his career, including the $2 million gold bathtub he bought for his first wife, actress Robin Givens, and a 420-horsepower Bentley Continental SC that came equipped with a phone, lamb's wool rugs, and a removable glass roof for $500,000. That's just one of many vehicles he purchased. Over the years, Tyson spent around $4.5 million on cars, including Ferraris, Lamborghinis, and Bentleys. In 2003, he filed for Chapter 11 bankruptcy, despite having earned nearly $400 million in his career up to that point.

Chad Johnson has never filed for bankruptcy, but according to the paperwork he entered in family court back in 2013 to have his child support amount lowered, his monthly expenses were $45,000 more than his monthly income. With $4.7 million in the bank, at this rate he'll be completely broke in less than ten years.

Sheryl Swoopes, the three-time gold medal Olympian and three-time WNBA MVP, has estimated lifetime earnings of $50 million. But in 2004, she filed for bankruptcy, claiming she owed nearly $750,000. She cited poor dealings by her money managers as the reason.

Former NFL quarterback Vince Young earned $34 million in six NFL seasons. He last played for a team in 2011, yet in 2013 he filed for Chapter 11 bankruptcy, citing his inability to pay back a $1.8 million loan that he took out during the 2011 NFL player lockout. The interest had caused that debt to grow to $2.5 million, but having been paid so much over the previous few years, he probably shouldn't have had to even take out that loan.

All of these athletes earned millions of dollars, yet let it slip away within a few short years. In all of these cases, better money management would not only have steered them away from their money mistakes but also could've helped them to gain financial freedom, which is the ultimate goal.

I am writing this book because I want to help you reach that ultimate goal of financial freedom. I played in the NBA for just over a decade, and because I managed my finances properly I am able to enjoy a lifetime of financial freedom. When I was drafted by the NBA my basic financial philosophy was that I would save as much money as possible during my career, in an attempt to have guaranteed, tax-free income for the rest of my life. After I got my first contract, I forced myself into thinking that there would not be another one. This made me craft a financial picture that allowed me to live within my means so that, even if my career ended in my rookie year, I would have enough money to live decently.

One of my goals was that I wanted minimal debt when I left the NBA. To this end, I wanted to keep my home, which meant I had to make financial arrangements to pay it off before my contract with the NBA expired. I purchased cars outright. I paid for my family's education. My rule was, everything I could afford in its entirety, I paid for in full.

I believe you can have the same financial freedom. I am composing this book with athletes in mind, but my primary goal is to share financial knowledge with everyone. While you may not be living the dream life of sports stars, I will show you that excessive materialism is not the key to happiness or financial freedom. You have to work with your money to make it work for you.

While I was on the NBA payroll, I consulted with professionals to figure out the best ways to invest my money, save, and still maintain a decent lifestyle. I wasn't concerned with wearing flashy jewelry, which was a big deal with basketball players during the era in which I played. I didn't care what others thought of me when I drove a Toyota 4Runner my rookie year. It was a vehicle that I could comfortably afford. I didn't enjoy the NBA any less, and I didn't enjoy driving any less.

I actually believe that living within my means has made me happier. So much so, that after retirement, when I became the director of player development for the Orlando Magic, I integrated financial literacy and awareness into the team's existing program. I regularly met with young players about their finances and was able to help these twenty- and twenty-one-year-olds make wise decisions with their income, which often rivals the salaries of big corporate CEOs. I couldn't tell you how many times I sat down with players and explained the importance of proper money management, because unfortunately they had never been taught anything about handling their finances.

In *Winning the Money Game*, I present important financial advice to help you avoid the financial fouls of athletes. I want to see you achieve financial success. While you, more than likely, earn a lot less than average pro athletes, the simple money management lessons that they should apply to save and grow their fortunes will work for you as well. Basic money principles apply no matter how much or how little money you earn.

In the pages that follow, I will explain how to manage your income so that you attain your goals. I'm talking about monetary goals as well as life goals. I want you to be able to manage your money in a way, right now, that will later allow you to enjoy the things in life that you want.

This invaluable book explores all the important areas you and athletes may find troublesome—from taxes to alimony, from child support to protecting your credit, and so much more. I explain the obligation of filing taxes on time and the consequences when you fail to pay.

Both getting married and getting divorced can impact your wallet negatively, depending on how you choose to deal with the events. The chapter on marriage and divorce will help you to protect your wealth and take care of your partner and children during the union or the unfortunate breakup.

Medical costs soar higher and higher each year, and in America health insurance is not guaranteed. For many individuals and families, a medical emergency could send them into bankruptcy. This handy book will show you how to prepare for emergencies.

To bring these issues to the forefront in a concrete manner, I present Big Baller Tom and Steady John. Through their financial decisions, you will be able to see on a spreadsheet the difference between living an excessive lifestyle and making smart decisions to live within your means.

Winning the Money Game features true, real-life stories about athletes' abuse of money, revealing their financial irresponsibility, as well as a few stories of financial success. These examples illustrate positive and negative actions. They highlight a lack of financial literacy; overspending on luxury items; expensive, large entourages; poor management of gifts for family and friends; bad business investments; gambling debts; excessive child support for illegitimate kids; and try-ing to jive Uncle Sam. These problems could be eradicated if athletes were to take control of their personal life the same way they take control of their destiny as athletes.

But make no mistake: This book is for everyone—not only pro athletes and celebrities. Whether you're a teenager just learning about finances, a college student with your first credit card, an entry-level professional earning your first real paycheck, or a parent looking for creative tools to help edu-cate your children about money, this entertaining book will put you on the fast track to financial success.

I know many athletes and friends who are living paycheck to paycheck because of their lack of financial knowledge. But it's a difficult way to live. It's easier to take the road that will allow your money to work for you. Too often, we believe it is completely acceptable to get paid every week, spend all of our money, and then wait until the next check comes. This is no way to live. That is a humdrum existence that keeps you chained to a desk or counter or whatever furniture your job requires. Let's enjoy a life of financial freedom by simply taking control of our finances. *Winning the Money Game* will show you how to be a winner!

WINNING
THE
MONEY GAME

CHAPTER ONE

PLAY TO WIN THE GAME

WHAT IS THE VALUE OF MONEY?

*F*or the love of money is the root of all evil. When you truly believe this statement, it will help you to prevent making money decisions that will impact your life negatively. This statement does not imply that you should not aspire to earn a lot of money. It is saying: Do not let money blind you. Do not put yourself in a position where you would sacrifice your morality for money. Money is not the root of all evil—being in love with it is.

The reality is, money is a necessity. You cannot live without it. The important thing is how you live with your money. When handled correctly, your money should be working for you. It should be viewed as nothing more than a tool to get you where you want to be in life. Your money should be respected and saved, not thrown away on lavish expenses.

The purpose of money is to put you in a position to provide for your basic needs—food, shelter, and clothing. When you manage your money properly, you will have the money to address your needs. You will also have extra money. This surplus is what allows you to define and enjoy your life.

Not having money is a serious problem. It contributes to stress and instability in your life. It impacts every decision you make. Do I wait in the freezing rain for the bus or can I afford to take a taxi? Should I take this new job with less security because I will make more week to week?

This is what happened to me: I hurt my knee. I was enjoying a wonderful, steady career when my knee went out. It was a career-ending injury, and it was difficult to say goodbye to a profession that I loved, that I had spent nearly my entire life perfecting. If I'd had to worry about the stress of not having saved enough money to maintain my lifestyle, the decision to retire would have been that much more difficult. After knee surgery, rehab, and the realization that I was never going back to playing, I had an incredible feeling of satisfaction that I had managed my money properly. Taking control of your money can make a huge difference in your life, no matter how much you are working with.

Like most National Basketball Association (NBA) players, Ulysses "Junior" Bridgeman didn't come from money. He grew up in East Chicago, Indiana, where his father was a steelworker. After he led his high school team to the 1971 Indiana state championship, Louisville offered him a basketball scholarship. When he was a senior, his Cardinals went to the National Collegiate Athletic Association (NCAA) Final Four, and he was taken with the eighth pick of the NBA Draft shortly after. Bridgeman played twelve seasons in the league: ten with the Milwaukee Bucks and two with the Los Angeles Clippers. He averaged 13.6 points per game despite coming off the bench for most of his career. For Milwaukee, he made a franchise-record 711 appearances.

Playing in the NBA, or in any professional sport, affords you the opportunity to meet powerful people: businessmen, bankers, and others you might never have come in contact with otherwise. Bridgeman, who graduated with a degree in psychology, used his time as president of the National Basketball Players Association (NBPA) to learn about business. The time he spent in collective-bargaining meetings with the owners was invaluable. He wanted to learn about business, and he was getting an education right there. Bridgeman, whose highest NBA salary was $350,000 a year, presided over the union at a time when player salaries averaged $600,000. He retired in 1987 at age thirty-three.

By April of the following year, he'd bought five Wendy's franchises, all in the Milwaukee area. Junior clearly was smart enough to not have wasted his money, because banks don't just loan money to people with no capital. With the stores up and running, Bridgeman jumped in with both feet, learning everything he could about the business. He flipped burgers, made fries, mopped floors, and even closed the stores at night. His learning the business by investing time and money eventually enabled all five of those stores to double their sales, and now they each pull in more than $1.5 million annually.

Bridgeman wasn't just sitting on his hands all that time. While those stores were increasing their revenue, he was out acquiring more. Today his company, Bridgeman Foods, owns 195 stores and is the second-largest Wendy's franchise owner in the country. Besides Wendy's, Bridgeman owns 125 Chili's restaurants, 45 Fannie May chocolate stores, and all kinds of other retail franchises. He employs nearly ten thousand people, and his net worth fluctuates between $200 million and $400 million.

Junior Bridgeman had a goal and got there by saving and managing his money well. He is now living a life of financial freedom. Isn't that what the American Dream is all about? It takes money to make money, so while you are able to earn an income, you have got to be smart with the money you have coming in. No matter how much or how little money you may have, you can manage it so that by the time you retire, you not only never have to work another day but you probably enjoy a pretty nice life.

Living financially free means that you're not worried about paying your cable bill or being evicted. Most people spend a good portion of their time figuring out which bill they're not going to pay this month so that they can catch up on another. The problem is, the following month, something else will have to get skipped to make up for the last unpaid bill. Robbing Peter to pay Paul is a never-ending cycle.

Everybody pays rent or makes a mortgage payment, and that's usually one's largest expense. Beyond that, there are the standard utilities such as electricity, gas, phone, and cable. I suppose you could include Wi-Fi and cell phone bills as part of the standard these days, too. If you own your home, you have to pay property taxes. Do you have a car? You have to make that payment every month as well. That's a lot of juggling. Wouldn't it be much simpler to put all of your bills on auto-pay and not have to worry about them at all? Financially free people can do that. It is a way to simplify one's life.

Money is also a safety net, because it allows you to handle emergencies. If a roof has too much snow on it and comes crashing in, a financially stable person is able to deal with this without too many complications. He calls a roofer, has him do the necessary repairs, then pays the bill. If you find yourself with a sunken roof and are not financially responsible—don't have the six months' worth of mortgage payments sitting in the bank, or don't have the proper home insurance—you are in a tough situation. Immediately, you have to figure out where your family will stay while you determine how you will get the money to repair the roof. Most likely, your solution will involve going further into debt.

In short, taking care of your finances offers you peace of mind—you do not have to worry about having enough money to pay your bills and live a respectable lifestyle.

At just six feet tall, Allen Iverson led the 2001 Philadelphia 76ers to the NBA Finals, winning one game before falling to the Kobe Bryant–led Los Angeles Lakers. However, his off-court issues with money are as well documented as his feats on the court. AI was an All-Star eleven times in fifteen seasons. He was Rookie of the Year, was named MVP, and led the league in scoring four times. He was well compensated for being one of the most talented players in basketball as well as one of the largest ticket draws, earning $154.5

million in salary over his career. Besides that, his numerous endorsements pushed his career earnings to more than $200 million.

Allen was known for traveling with a large entourage. Writers, workers, and fans around his team and the league always put the number of crew members at around fifty. I've seen him with groups of people, but never that many. Either way, any athlete traveling with a large entourage is spending big money on them, trust me. Allen was taking exotic vacations, buying luxury cars, and blowing millions in Atlantic City and Las Vegas. With all of that, it only makes sense that by 2012, when he was just one year removed from the basketball court, it was revealed that his monthly income was $62,500, but his monthly expenses were $360,000. The majority of his expenses were paying back various creditors and mortgages on several homes.

In fairness, he does have a $30 million trust fund that he can't touch until 2030. At that point, he'll be fifty-five years old, and hopefully a little wiser about what he does with his money.

It's not only basketball players who fall victim to bad money decisions. Former heavyweight boxing champion Evander Holyfield blew through the $230 million he made in his career and is now deep in debt, owing hundreds of thousands of dollars in taxes. After winning bronze in the 1984 Olympics, Holyfield turned pro and over the next two decades accumulated a 42–10–2 record, with 27 knockouts. Along the way he had wins over such big-time boxers as Larry Holmes, Riddick Bowe, George Foreman, and Mike

Tyson—twice, including the infamous battle in which Tyson bit off a piece of Evander's ear.

In 2008, Evander found himself in trouble with a bank, and it foreclosed on his 54,000-square-foot mansion in Atlanta. The 109-room estate sat on 234 acres and cost more than $1 million a year to maintain, a real drain on Holyfield's bank account. As a result of his debts, many of his personal belongings—including his Olympic medal, championship belts, and even the robes he wore at matches—have been sold at auction.

When people get sidetracked and start spending money on unnecessary items, only trouble can follow. That $230 million should have been enough to take care of Evander and his immediate family for generations, but due to poor money management, that is not what his legacy will be, and no one is hurt by that more than the athlete's family.

Situations like Iverson's and Holyfield's are what make outside observers think that money is bad, but that's just not so. It's the mistakes people make—especially flashy, shiny mistakes that others can see around their neck or in their driveway—that in the long run cause them to go broke. When you see a person who's lost all his money and appears to be worse off than he was before he ever had a dime, the immediate reaction is to blame the money. But the money is not to blame—ignorance about what to do with it is.

For pro players, all of whom retire at a young age, money allows for options once you take off the uniform. Money gives you time. With all of your needs taken care of, you have time to figure out what it is you really want to do with the next phase of your life. You should really plan for this day long before it actually comes and hopefully have a smooth and immediate transfer into your new profession. However, if you do not make a smooth and immediate transfer, you can still live comfortably until you are ready and able to make the next move. Having that time and security will also help you to make the best decision. There will be no pressure to take the first available opportunity; you can wait it out until the right thing comes along. If your anticipated next step requires any additional education, you can afford it. Again, money allows you to be free.

Jonathan Bender, who was never a big star in the NBA, struggled through rookie and second seasons that were lackluster at best, but that didn't stop the Pacers from offering him a four-year, $28 million contract in October 2002. In 1999, after breaking Michael Jordan's scoring record in the McDonald's High School All-American Game, Bender decided to go straight to the NBA, figuring that college would only lower his draft stock. That was probably a pretty good decision. Bender had bad knees, which were only getting worse, so he figured that playing ball at college would make him less likely to be drafted by an NBA team. Arthroscopic surgery performed in the summer of 2003 was supposed to repair the cartilage in his knee, but the operation didn't quite work and he played only a few games after that, before retiring at twenty-five.

One day while hanging out in the park, Bender came up with a training and rehab device that he thought could help him and others like him to walk better, in turn helping with workouts. He spent the next two years testing it out, mostly by letting his friends use it during workouts. Once he got the thumbs-up from them, he took it to research doctors at Purdue University, who confirmed that it eased pressure on the knees, built strength in the hamstrings and calves, and offered lower-joint relief.

After working out with the device for a year himself, he felt that the true test would be his ability to make an NBA comeback. Three years after he had last played in an NBA game, he contacted Donnie Walsh, who had been the general manager (GM) when he was in Indiana. Walsh was with the Knicks and invited Bender to try out. He made the team and played in twenty-five games—but more importantly, he confirmed to himself that he had built up unbelievable strength in his lower body. The team invited him to come back but he declined, opting to instead improve on his invention, find a manufacturer, and figure out how to sell it.

In 2013, Bender's JBIT MedPro went on sale to the public. He got it into several stores and had significant online sales, earning more than $500,000 in his first year. Today, he is still running a one-man business, handling everything, including overseeing the outside companies that fulfill orders.

Bender was sitting on $30 million when he retired, and having that money put away is the main reason he was able to first take a year to come up with his invention, then spend another two years testing it out, and finally invest another year in the last part of his test, an NBA comeback. Now, Bender is running a company and doing exactly what he wants to do, and was able get there because of the freedom that his money provided. Money offers you choices.

Saving money shouldn't be a foreign concept, but for too many people, it is. Remember, saved money grows while spent money just disappears. The more your money grows, the better off you will be. While you may need to make some sacrifices early in your adult life, you should be able to have your money working to make your life comfortable within a few short years.

In 2013, the average American household was worth $81,400. Of course, that's not all cash, but that's for another discussion. A closer look at the numbers reveals that the average household had a value of $141,900, while the average urban household had a net worth of just $11,000.

As a result of generations of this kind of disparity, money has taken on a special meaning for athletes from urban areas. They tend to view money as a status symbol. While the freedom of not worrying about bills is something everyone wants to enjoy, for athletes, it's much more. Money shows others that you've made it or that you've exceeded what others expected of you. Urban areas place a much larger value on money than others, feeling as though money cures all ills. But it is not a magic potion. These athletes believe that having money levels the playing field, but it does not. It may get you in the door at an exclusive restaurant, but it won't force the other diners to socialize with you.

Very simply, for athletes coming from an urban background, money has become more than just currency—it has become a symbol of achievement. Young people believe that it will give them a leg up in society, and respect from their community and others.

What is the role that you want money to play in your life? You can always be in debt, scrambling to pay back credit cards and not quite having enough money for the things you need, or you can have enough money to not have to worry about bills, emergencies, or anything else. Money is valuable for your peace of mind, as well as for affording you options in your life. Smart decisions and wise saving will get you the money, power, and respect that you want and deserve.

CHAPTER TWO

GET OFF THE SIDELINE

BECOMING INVOLVED WITH YOUR FINANCES

Professional athletes are the most fortunate of souls. By virtue of making it to the highest level of their sport, athletes can become millionaires overnight and ensure their financial security for the rest of their lives. Many Americans spend their entire lives trying to figure out a way to make money and get rich, but athletes are already there. Pro athletes know how to get rich; the problem is that most of them don't know how to stay rich.

The best way to stay on top of your money is to stay on top of your money. In other words, you should all get personally involved in overseeing and managing your finances. If money is important to you (and with the way our society operates, it should be), you have to put in the work. Just as with anything else, the more you know, the better off you are. You have to spend some time learning about your finances by reading books, taking courses, talking to bankers or tax consultants, or even watching financial shows on television. This is the largest responsibility anyone has before he or she pulls in the first paycheck.

In the case of professional athletes, this is especially troubling, because before they get to the point where they are making millions, they've most likely put in fifteen years of practices and workouts. They and their parents have invested money in equipment and time going to practices and games, traveling the Amateur Athletic Union (AAU) circuit, and handling commitments to their school team(s). They may have altered their bodies by changing their eating habits in order to gain or lose weight, or got on some workout regimen to build muscle mass. So, for them to finally get to the level where they're earning millions, only to lose it all in a few years simply because they wouldn't take the time to learn about their finances, is mind-boggling.

The same is true for most people earning an average income. The fact that you have picked up *Winning the Money Game* shows that you are likely concerned about using your money to set yourself up for life and be able to retire in comfort. Although pro athletes make more money than most, the financial pitfalls they encounter are similar to those of everyday earners.

Throughout my career in the NBA, I've seen more players refuse to get involved with their finances than I can count. It's not necessarily because they don't want to—it's because they're afraid of venturing into areas where they don't know everything . . . or, in most cases, anything. Many people don't know all they should about finances. I don't recall a course in personal finance taught in schools. Your parents most likely don't have all the information they should. So, when and where do you learn?

The NBPA holds mandatory meetings about players' finances, but they're often highly ineffective. These meetings are not the proper setting to discuss individuals' specific issues anyway, because they aren't private and no one wants to ask questions and sound uninformed in front of teammates and friends. Guys will come to the meetings straight from practice, still trying to catch their breath, as NBA and players' union officials alike bend their ears back not only about financial issues but about gambling and sexually transmitted diseases as well. On top of that, the information they offer on money matters is too general.

There's always a good mixture of players in the meetings. There'll be first- and second-year players who have yet to open their first checking account and are completely overwhelmed by all the information being thrown at them, alongside veterans who yawn and entertain themselves on their smartphones for the entire meeting because they feel like they've heard it all before. There are some players, young and old, who soak up all the information and go out and use the advice, but the majority do not.

Across the table are the NBA reps, who are there to help, but are also concerned about exposing themselves to lawsuits. To avoid this, they speak in very general terms, as opposed to telling players exactly what kind of accounts they should be setting up for retirement, providing details about life insurance, suggesting methods to ensure their taxes are paid, or even offering information about creating a will. This general information isn't good enough, especially for the younger players, who each have specific issues that need to be addressed.

During my rookie year I found these meetings excruciating. I was a basketball player, and all I wanted to do was play basketball; I didn't want to figure out the differences between municipal bonds and regular bonds or mutual funds. But I matured quickly, because it's critical to be involved with what's happening to your money, and education is the key. You are off to a good start by purchasing this book, but there are some others that I would highly recommend, such as *Rich Dad, Poor Dad*, by Robert Kiyosaki; *Financially Stupid People Are Everywhere: Don't Be One of Them*, by Jason Kelly; and *Money Players*, by Marc Isenberg. These books, like mine, offer varying perspectives on the fundamentals of finances, assisting you in setting short- and long-term goals. We want to catch you before you attempt to buy a Bentley or a Rolex with your first paycheck!

There are plenty of financial literacy courses. A simple Google search will lead you to free financial courses online, via downloadable software, and classes that actually meet in person. In person or online, classes permit you to get your specific questions answered.

Money issues are commonly discussed on television as well. On *Mad Money*, while Jim Cramer is giving his stock tips, he is also breaking down how these companies work and why their stocks are going up or down, speaking in terms that most people can understand.

You can learn a lot from *The Suze Orman Show*, too. She tells people what they need to hear even when they don't want to hear it. On one occasion, she explained to a caller that based on the woman's and her husband's income and expenses, it didn't make sense for them to have a baby at that time. That's not what the caller wanted to hear. Imagine being told that you shouldn't have a child when you and your spouse are ready and primed. Suze explained that they were emotionally ready, but not financially prepared. Suze can explain why you aren't financially prepared for that Porsche Panamera, either.

Many people seem fearful of tackling financial concepts. But just like you know a lot about sports while there are others who don't know much at all, it's just a matter of immersing yourself in it.

For young athletes, there are many opportunities to help them get started on managing their finances. Each year, the NBA and NBPA host a Rookie Symposium that helps the new players understand some of the challenges they'll encounter throughout their basketball career. Through various panel discussions, workshops, and other events, issues such as sex education, handling the media, and, yes, financial literacy are presented. However, judging from *Sports Illustrated*'s 2009 estimation that 60 percent of NBA players are broke within five years of retiring from the game, this effort seems to be falling short.

If you talk to veterans around the league, a lot of them have made the same observation: They don't believe that young athletes listen to the financial advice they're given. A

large percentage of the players who come into the league had no money before they got there, so when they receive those big paychecks, all they want to do is spend. They don't realize how important it is to save money, though occasionally you come across a young player who does understand or who at least has parents whom he listens to and who are thinking in his best interest.

Michael Carter-Williams, who was drafted by the Philadelphia 76ers with the eleventh pick in the 2013 NBA Draft, signed a rookie contract that paid him $4.5 million over his first season. With the help of his mother, he decided to put just about all of it into a trust fund that he can't touch for three years. This was a smart move, because it will assure an income, and a pretty good one, for years into the future. In the meantime, he is living on the money he makes from his endorsement deals with Nike and Panini trading cards. Since NBA rookie contracts are capped, their second contract is the one where they can make some real money. So, there's still a chance for Carter-Williams to make it rain in the clubs, although something tells me he's not going to.

There is nothing more important than managing your money so that your money is working for you. As you write each check, you get a picture of what's happening with your finances. The act of signing a check makes the payment real. You really feel like you're spending some of your hard-earned money when you physically write out that check and sign it.

I remember once writing a check for my brother's school tuition. The check was for $26,000. When I signed it, I almost had a nervous breakdown. However, that was nothing

compared with the time I had to write a check for $200,000 to the IRS. I immediately fired my certified public accountant (CPA) and hired another, with whom I have been for the last several years. The first time we met, I told the new CPA that I don't like paying huge tax liabilities and that I hate surprises. Then I asked him not to let that happen to me again.

Writing out a check for $200,000 will make you realize the importance of having a certified professional handling your taxes. Now, if you just have one job, especially if you're new to the work world or don't have much income, you could just walk into an H&R Block or Jackson Hewitt office during tax season—the beginning of January through April 15—and have them do your taxes for you. They will only charge you a small fee and, in addition to saving you time and labor, will probably save you money. But later on, when you begin making more, or maybe start a small business, it would be in your best interest to hire a CPA, because you are going to need to consult him throughout the year, not just during tax season.

Professional athletes should think of themselves as small businesses from the day they sign their first contract, and should hire a CPA right away. This is the person who will stay on top of your money and your taxes. He makes sure you're paying the proper amount to the government, but will also try to find ways for you to legally pay less. CPAs offer advice on income tax and business tax strategies, assist with personal and business tax planning, and prepare income tax returns. A CPA can also represent individuals before government agencies at federal, state, and local levels.

This process is a little more difficult for high-income earners, as they need to actually build a financial team. In addition to a CPA, a high earner will need to hire a financial consultant and a lawyer, and may even bring a trusted confidant into the loop. For pro athletes, an agent may have to be part of this team as well.

A financial adviser can guide you on whether you can put all of your money away, like Michael Carter-Williams did, or just a small portion. He'll tell you if it should go into an annuity or a trust. Your consultant will know better than you if you should buy a house with a fixed-rate mortgage, pay cash straight out, or just rent for now. Financial consultants are well versed in insurance matters and can tell you the proper insurance to get. In addition to a pension and a 401(k), there are several different types of retirement accounts you can establish, and your consultant will be able to help you there as well. Essentially, the consultant will keep you on track to meet your life's goals.

When I signed my first NBA contract and looked for a financial adviser, I stayed away from mom-and-pop financial firms because I was worried about being able to get my money back if they made a mistake. A larger firm has more resources and, if it were to mismanage my money and I had to sue, it would no doubt be able to repay me. But that doesn't mean a mom-and-pop organization won't work for you. I researched different companies, while looking for someone within those companies who could talk to me one-on-one and explain things in a way I could understand. I talked in depth with each company and each consultant about my financial goals. As I interviewed several financial companies, I asked questions about their fees and the history of their company. I also requested references, and checked them thoroughly.

After I secured a financial consultant, he presented me with a plan on ways to invest my existing funds. It is important to educate yourself as much as possible before hiring anyone. Don't be intimidated by financial professionals. We earn our money by playing a sport, and that's what we are trained for. You may earn your money working in a bank or a hospital or as a garbage collector. Financial consultants earn their money by crunching numbers—that's their training. Financial advisers have no right to look down on you for something you're not yet trained in. One of the reasons a financial consultant is hired is to teach you everything you need to know about managing your finances. Don't feel insecure because you're not an expert. You're smart enough to seek assistance.

A lawyer is necessary for dealing with a real estate deal, whether it's your own home or some sort of investment property. He also deals with issues with contracts and would handle your money were you to become incapacitated. In general, a lawyer keeps an eye on the contractual and legal requirements for all of an athlete's professional endeavors.

Once your financial team is established, someone you trust and know personally should be brought into the mix. This person should always have your best interest at heart. She is not compensated and should not have a stake in your finances. This trusted confidant is included in all meetings and is aware of everything that's going on in your financial camp, whether you're investing in a business or opening a new checking account. Your confidant is your eyes and ears. This person's sole responsibility is to protect you by asking the tough questions and by challenging your financial team.

For me, finding a trusted confidant was easy: I called on the services of my stepdad. His job was simply to be a pain in the ass. One of the reasons I chose him is that he is an economics professor at Colgate University. He once told me that when it comes to my money, there should be absolutely no fear in asking where it goes.

If you don't happen to have a stepfather who's an economics professor, then you may want to look to a college professor, a mentor, a religious leader, a former coach, or even a former teammate to be that personal confidant on your financial team. It just needs to be someone with whom you have a history and whom you trust implicitly. Ideally, confidants should be happy and successful in their own life and not need anything from you. They are there to ask the right questions, not manage the portfolio. They shouldn't have any stake in the outcome other than a personal interest in your success. If you don't have anyone you think can do this, you need to start seeking out a mentor or identifying people who could serve in this role down the line.

Building a team like this is the only way to make sure your money is protected. You *must* require absolute transparency from the team members and ask every question you can think of. Your financial team should send you a report every month, followed up by a meeting to make sure everyone is working toward the same goals. It's your money, and it's your job to stay on top of it.

When an athlete hires an agent, he is bringing in the person who will handle all of his sports dealings, from negotiating contracts to helping him get acclimated to a new city after a trade. An agent's primary responsibility is to get his client to sign a contract with a team. If the agent is good or if he represents a lot of players, he can use his influence or leverage some of the other players he has to get more incentives or more money out of the team. Agents also secure marketing deals. They are the ones who negotiate with Nike or Buick or McDonald's to secure ad campaigns and shoe lines. This is where the agents make their money. NBA contracts are regulated by the NBPA, so an agent can only take a maximum of 4 percent of the contract's value as a commission; however, with marketing deals, there is no regulation, so agents routinely charge clients as much as 25 percent for securing a deal. Since agents are usually lawyers, they often handle paternity suits or any other kind of lawsuit that may be served on a player, too.

As I continued my career in the NBA, I became more and more aware of where my money was going. I began to monitor my financial team and make adjustments when necessary. When you're making a lot of money, and want it to grow, you must be involved in your finances. The more you practice managing your money and your financial team, the better your results. Ask your financial team to answer every single question that comes to mind and to define every term you don't know. They work for you. The more you practice this particular skill, the richer you will be—in many ways.

If you think someone is messing with your money, you have the right to audit that person. In fact, it's good to audit your financial team regularly even when things seem to be okay. The NBPA has resources available upon request to audit people who work for NBA players. I took advantage of this service and audited my financial team at least once a year, just to keep them on their toes. As a result, they always knew I was paying attention to them and treated me with respect.

If you're not at the level where you need a team, you should still check up on your CPA to make sure he's not stealing money or simply making honest mistakes; either way, you'd be losing out. Most people are not members of the NBA players' union and therefore don't have access to audit resources on request, but you can show your financial reports to an independent consultant or a bank and let them evaluate what's going on. You're never going to know how safe you are unless you let outside, third-party professionals audit whoever is handling your money.

An audit takes all the decisions your financial team makes during the course of a year and hands them over to a third party to independently critique and evaluate. The auditors examine individual tax returns and other documents. They evaluate the efficiency of your financial profile and portfolio.

You should audit your accountant, your lawyer, your financial team . . . your mother. You should audit anyone to whom you give money or who has authority over your affairs. A financial audit of your team offers additional proof that your faith in them is justified—or not. Listen, your mother should be happy that her son audits her. It shows that he is fiscally aware and taking steps to ensure his long-term financial stability.

During my time as a player rep and then vice president with the NBPA, I saw enormous amounts of fraud perpetrated on athletes by various financial companies. They overcharged massively. Sometimes the companies in question weren't even financial firms—they simply took the money to another institution. They charged athletes anywhere from 3 to 5 percent of their total contract while they did nothing.

―――――――――――――― TIPS ――――――――――――――

1. At the minimum, learn the basics about your money.
2. Pay attention to the advice you're given.
3. Hire a CPA or a financial team.
4. Bring in a trusted friend to keep an eye on your financial team.
5. Ask questions about anything you don't understand.
6. Sign every check yourself. That way you will see every dollar as it goes out and will know where your money is being spent.
7. Audit anyone who is dealing with your money.

Even after taking great care in selecting my financial team, I learned that it is not an exact science. My first tax consultant turned out to not be ideal for me. His firm was very large, and while he kept my money safe, I didn't feel I was being given the kind of attention I needed. I fired that firm and selected another that took more time to explain its transactions and recommendations. When it came time to choose a lawyer, I asked people in my network, including my teammates and front office executives, for referrals. I took especially seriously the advice from veterans on my team—at least the ones who had managed their finances well. And, I'm happy to say, my choice of lawyers worked out very well for me.

CHAPTER THREE

GOING FOR THE GOLD

MANAGING YOUR INCOME

"It's official. Pride 2 the side. just filled out a application
at Home Depot. Lockout aint a game."

Former Boston Celtics guard Delonte West tweeted the
above as the 2011 NBA lockout was just getting under way.
Despite having made more than $14 million during his
seven-year career prior to 2011, West needed to bring in a
paycheck to make ends meet. He never got the job at Home
Depot, but he did end up working at a local furniture store in
Maryland, doing truck deliveries. Delonte, who has bipolar
disorder, even tweeted a picture of himself on the delivery
truck with other workers. After the lockout ended and paychecks started rolling in again, there were rumors that he was
sleeping in the Dallas Mavericks practice facility because he
had no place to live in the city.

To understand why highly paid athletes often fall into

financial distress, let's start with the basic concept of income versus expenses. When players turn pro, they are usually overwhelmed by their drastic increase in income, to the extent that expenses become an afterthought. As difficult as it is to believe, there are a large number of current NBA players living paycheck to paycheck. The only reason they're not completely broke is that they have guaranteed contracts.

Let's take Eddy Curry, for example. In the midst of a $60 million contract, he was having financial difficulties because he had purchased a $4.5 million mansion and hired a $6,000-a-month chef. He was forced to take out a $580,000 loan with an 85 percent interest rate. Other outlays included $30,000 in household expenses and $17,000 in allowances, which went to relatives or to his entourage.

The expenses-as-afterthought concept also applies to kids straight out of college and into a $30,000-a-year job. At twenty-three years old, young adults living on their own outside a college environment can feel as though they've made it. But they haven't made it. They are far from making it. What they should be doing at this point is making a plan for their money so they don't start off by wasting valuable income that can only help them later in life. Just like a rookie athlete making $900,000 in his first year, some pros getting $30,000 at their first job could get the idea that they have enough money to freely spend, spend, spend. They don't.

What you may not realize is that around 30 to 35 percent of that money is going to taxes. Of the remainder, you have to pay rent and utilities and you have to buy food and clothes.

Those are your basic necessities. Unfortunately, these necessities may take up the bulk of your entire annual salary. Let me explain a little further. In 2013, the median annual earnings for full-time working 25- to 32-year-olds with bachelor's degrees was $45,500, and for high school graduates it was $28,000. So, if we split that in half and assume you are earning $36,750 per year, based on a 40-hour workweek it breaks down to $17.67 per hour, or $706.80 each week. Assuming you pay a total of 30 percent of that to federal, state, and local (city or township) taxes, $212.04 will be deducted by your employer before you even see that check. Throw in an additional $10 for health insurance (this number could vary depending on your health care choices) and you will be bringing home $494.76 every Friday. Multiply that by four, and you earn $1,979.04 a month in take-home pay.

Now, with that in your pocket, how much is your rent—$700? What about the gas, water, and electric bills each month? Let's assume your utilities total $150. Don't forget about your cable and cell phone bills. Paying $100 a month for cable and $60 for your cell phone is a fairly low-end estimate. How much does it cost for you to commute to work? Let's say you live in a big city and buy an unlimited bus pass. That could run you around $90. Then you have to fill the refrigerator. If you live alone, you won't need much. Assuming that you cook rather than eat out every night, you could spend $400 on food each month.

Have you been keeping track? Monthly expenses come to $1,500. That's $1,500 out of the $1,979.04 that you bring home every month. That leaves you with $479.04, or $119.76

a week, that you can use for disposable income. However, that money isn't necessarily disposable. We haven't talked about clothes. You have to wear something, so you'll be using some of that money to purchase attire. Also, and as important as buying clothes, do you want to put any of that money away in a savings or retirement account? Do you want to invest any of it in the stock market?

You can see how easy it is for someone making $36,750 a year to overspend and blow his entire budget. But when one brings in millions and hasn't been educated in finances, he can blow his budget just as easily.

Allen Iverson, who made more than $200 million in salary and endorsements while playing for the Sixers, Nuggets, and Pistons, spent more than $254 million on cars, jewelry, and vacations.

Former Cleveland Browns quarterback Bernie Kosar earned around $19 million over his thirteen-year career and is said to have made much more after retiring from football, yet in 2009 he filed for bankruptcy, claiming over $19.5 million in debt. According to Kosar, he was too generous with his family and friends. According to his lawyer, the real estate bust took him down. According to his court filing, he still owed his ex-wife $3 million from their divorce settlement.

Jason Caffey, who raked in $30 million during his basketball career, claims that he is broke due to child support payments and bad investments.

Curt Schilling earned over $114 million in his twenty-year baseball career, yet he had to ask the Hall of Fame to return his infamous bloody sock so that he could sell it at auction to pay off some personal debts. The numbers go on and on and on.

Before we figure out ways to not lose all of your money, let's look at all of the various income sources you and an athlete can have.

CONTRACTS

Unlike professional football players, who have nonguaranteed contracts, most professional basketball players' contracts are guaranteed. This means that once you sign a contract with an NBA team, you will be paid that money come hell or high water. If a few years into your contract, the team feels as though you are not playing at the level you were when it agreed to pay you that money, it still has to pay you. If it decides to trade you to another team, the new team is forced to honor the remaining time on the contract that you signed with your original team. Basically, if you sign a deal for seven years and $25 million, at the end of seven years you will have been paid every cent of that money.

The NFL doesn't work the same way. When a football player signs a contract, it doesn't mean a whole lot. If he signs that deal for seven years and $25 million, there will generally be a signing bonus. If the bonus is $4 million, he will definitely get the four million plus whatever amount he is supposed to get in his first year. After that, an NFL team can cancel a contract at any time. So, if a player in his second year isn't playing up to his contract, the team can decide that it wants to tear up the contract and have him renegotiate a new contract for less money. If the player is unwilling to renegotiate, the team can just let him go, with no compensation.

If you're under contract with a company, it guarantees your income for a specified amount of time. An employment contract with a business is similar to a professional sports contract in that there is usually a defined amount of time you are guaranteed employment and a certain salary that is assigned, as well as other benefits and perks. In your contract you may want to negotiate terms that would not allow your salary to ever be below an equivalent employee's salary. There are lots of negotiation points that can go into a contract if you want to get creative—so many that some would-be employees even use a human resources lawyer to negotiate on their behalf.

Of course, there are a couple of immediate deductions that come out of an athlete's paycheck.

First, the government and state taxes take roughly 35 percent. The actual percentage depends on how much the athlete makes and his primary state of residence.

Second, due to a collective bargaining agreement between the NBA and the NBPA about how to share basketball-related income (BRI), all players' salaries combined total just about half of the money the NBA earns, which includes ticket sales, television contracts, concessions, parking, and arena advertising. Because of this, both parties agree to hold upward of 10 percent of what a player makes in an escrow account, in case at the end of the year players end up owing the league based on the agreed amount of the BRI for that season. This is called escrow withholding. At the end of the year, when the numbers are audited by an independent company, players may get back all or a portion of that 10 percent of their withholding, though it's rare that an athlete's money is fully returned.

In addition, some athletes pay a financial consultant about 2 percent of their revenue to manage their portfolio.

Despite all these expenses, a $20 million contract is still a $20 million contract. Most people would gladly accept the responsibilities that come with this income.

ENDORSEMENT DEALS

Big endorsement deals are what many who are not sports fans think of when they think of pro athletes' income. They may not know much about the game, but they know who the big stars are, simply because they pop up on television during nonsports programming, usually in a slickly produced ad pushing sneakers or cars.

The Clippers' Blake Griffin takes on the persona of a super-hero to sell Kia Optimas to low-end car buyers around the country. Tiger Woods was touting the quality of Buick automobiles, while Houston Texan linebacker J. J. Watt dances to promote Verizon Wireless.

Not long ago, tennis player Maria Sharapova signed a deal with Nike that will pay her $70 million over eight years, making her the highest-paid woman among athletes with endorsement deals. She will also receive a percentage of the sales of her product line. For men, endorsements seem to be even more lucrative, as $100 million over ten years seems to be some sort of standard deal. Damian Lillard from the Trail Blazers got that from Adidas, the Heat's Dwyane Wade agreed to the same deal from a Chinese shoe brand called Li-Ning, and pro golfer Rory McIlroy signed for those terms with Nike.

Beyond that, international soccer star David Beckham signed a lifetime contract with Adidas that will pay him $160 million; he collected $80 million up front. The oft-injured Derrick Rose of the Chicago Bulls has an Adidas deal worth $185 million over fourteen years, and there are incentives on top of that that could push his payout as high as $260 million. That still pales next to LeBron James's deal with Nike, which pays him $30 million a year. But even LeBron is looking up at the granddaddy of them all, Michael Jordan. Nike's deal with Jordan has been estimated to have paid him around $100 million in 2013, as sales of Jordan Brand products reached $2.7 billion that year.

Not every player receives financial endorsements. The larger endorsement deals go to the top players in the league like Shaquille O'Neal or Kevin Durant. You can find those players endorsing everything from fast food to audio equipment. Other players who may have a marketable personality can get smaller deals with a local car dealership or the like. Most players get in-kind deals with products like shoes and clothing from companies like Nike, Adidas, and Reebok.

Agents can take anywhere from 10 to 25 percent of a player's endorsement income, because unlike regular contracts these deals are not regulated by the league or the union. On a player's contract with his team, 4 percent is the maximum an agent can receive. For top players, the amount of money possible via endorsements dwarfs their NBA contracts. For example, LeBron James makes $50 to $80 million in endorsement deals each year. Meanwhile, his contract with the Heat was for $110 million for six years, or $18.3 million a year. With Cleveland he signed a two-year deal for $42.1 million.

LICENSING CHECK

Licensing is the practice of paying a business or other entity for the use of its name, logo, or likeness to promote some other product. The entity that owns the name, logo, or likeness is paid by the other party for its use. So, when a company produces kids' lunch boxes with Mickey Mouse on them, Disney is getting a check. The same is true with the NBA. When a company creates T-shirts with team logos, or specific players' jerseys, even in video games, the NBA gets paid. The money is split between the players and owners, and then the players divide their share equally. The amount of money made by the NBA for licensing varies from year to year, depending on the sales of NBA merchandise in a given year.

Every year, the NBA cuts each player a check for his share of merchandising revenues from hats, jackets, and all the other team goods that fans drop their hard-earned money on. This money is evenly distributed to every player in the league and is usually around $25,000 net. The gross amount is around $35,000, but the NBPA takes $10,000 for union dues. Unfortunately, the player will have to pay taxes on the entire $35,000, but with a smart CPA, he should be able to write off the $10,000 at the end of the year.

PER DIEM

This was by far one of my favorite perks of being in the NBA. On every road trip, players received $120 per day for food, even though the team serves meals at meetings, after games, and on plane trips. Many teams around the league will also provide food for players before and after practice to ensure they keep up with good nutrition. In other words, per diem essentially became pocket money.

Most players in the league use the per diem to buy clothes or a new iPod while they're on the road, but I went a different route. I would never spend my per diem. I would put it in an envelope and take it back home, where I had all the per diems from the entire season saved up. At the end of the year, that money would add up to $5,000 or $6,000. Using that money, I would visit a new country each year during the off-season. My "per diem vacations" included cruising the Mediterranean, touring England, and even dropping by for a visit to Morocco.

BASKETBALL CAMPS

Players can make quite a bit of money hosting summer basketball camps. Each camp event can bring in as much as $20,000 or more, depending on the player's stature. For example, a hometown hero may not be well known all over the country, but in his hometown he is a celebrity, and that's bankable. The player's team can also join with an individual player to organize basketball camps where the team does all the work and the player merely shows up and earns anywhere between $5,000 and $20,000 just for talking to the kids in the camp— offering encouragement, sharing life stories, and imparting some basketball skills.

401(K) PLAN

A 401(k) is a type of retirement plan subsidized by the U.S. government. The NBA has one of the most generous 401(k) plans in the country. If a player puts in the maximum allowable amount of $17,500 per year, the league will put about $23,500 per year into the player's retirement plan, for a total of $41,000 in retirement savings annually. Uncle Sam helps out by giving you a tax break for your contribution. In short, you are being paid to save.

The 401(k) retirement plans are a great deal: You get tax breaks when you put money in, and your money is put into stocks and bonds that (almost always) increase in value over time. For instance, if a basketball player were to put in just $17,500 per year for four years after turning pro at twenty, the NBA would match that contribution each year with its $23,500, and at a 5 percent annual gain the player would have well over $1.3 million in his account when he reached retirement age at fifty-nine and a half.

But as good as the NBA deal is, Major League Base-ball (MLB) and the National Football League (NFL) have it beat. While the NBA matches your $17,500 with $23,500, representing 140 percent of your contribution, the NFL and MLB each represent 200 percent of their players' 401(k) contributions.

Most large companies have 401(k) plans, and you should definitely take advantage of it. But don't expect to get 200 percent in matching funds, or even 140 percent, from your company. Most companies do around 50 percent, if they match your contribution at all. You can certainly find com-panies that do 100 percent, but unless you can put it over the fence like Mike Trout or outmuscle a defender to catch a pass like Calvin Johnson, don't look for 200 percent matching. If you're not sure if your company offers a 401(k), check with its human resources department.

When the NBA first rolled out its retirement plan, a lot of players were skeptical and refused to participate. I remember spending almost an hour trying to convince a player that it was not a scam and that he was receiving free money to save.

PENSION

If a player stays in the league for at least three years, he can become part of the pension pool when he retires. This is in addition to his 401(k). The minimum benefit for a player who retires (or starts collecting his retirement benefits) at sixty-two is $56,988 per year, and believe me, you will be hard-pressed to find another company that pays out this much after only three years of service, with one exception again being baseball. It takes just forty-three days of service for an MLB player to qualify for the minimum $34,000 a year at age sixty-two. The maximum benefit for an NBA player is $195,000, and it takes eleven years of playing to qualify for this benefit. MLB players need to play ten years to become eligible for the maximum. You should investigate your company's pension plan, as they vary considerably.

MEDICAL REIMBURSEMENTS

The medical reimbursement account is another source of income. The league contributes upward of $20,000 into a medical reimbursement account for every year an athlete plays. The money is used for medical expenses for players and their families. By the time I retired, after thirteen years in the league, I had more than $300,000 in my account to help with all my current and future medical expenses, as well as insurance payments. Since my retirement, I have needed surgery on my knees (a knee injury ended my career) and have had other lingering issues from all those years of playing. Health care is one of the most important things you can have in retirement. Whether you're a pro athlete or not, you're going to have health issues as you get into your older years. Contributing into a fund while you're still working to help pay for medical expenses when you're not is a good way to protect yourself.

PLAYOFF BONUS

You always see players go all out to make the playoffs. When it comes down to the end of the season, players will give that extra effort to chase down a loose ball, or maybe you'll see one dive into the fans' seats to save a ball that was going out of bounds. Everyone wants to win a championship, and you can't do that without making the playoffs first. But what most fans don't realize is that players are compensated for making the playoffs, and the teams that go deeper into the postseason earn even more. Each of the players on a playoff team is given a check for $5,000, plus an additional $5,000 per round that the team wins. In addition, there are bonuses for achievements such as best record in the conference and most overall wins.

SAVINGS PLAN

Under the latest collective bargaining agreement (CBA), the NBA and the NBPA have agreed to a new savings plan for NBA players. The players' union is planning to buy annuities. These annuities are designed to accept money from an individual, grow it, and then make a stream of payments to that individual at a later time. To help ensure that they save some money, people usually take these payments after retirement. With this plan, the NBA and the union are trying to deal with the epidemic of players going broke shortly after their playing days are over by forcing them to save through wage garnishments. Currently, this plan has yet to go into effect; details of its implementation are still being discussed, because financial advisers have suggested that annuities are not necessarily in the best interest of the players.

You may very well have some supplemental income streams in your profession that you could take advantage of. Some of these streams will be in the form of money and others will offer you ways to save money. For instance, you might negotiate for freebies: a parking spot, perhaps, or additional work space.

Most large corporations offer a 401(k) plan to their employees, and I highly recommend that you take advantage of this program. You should always save the maximum amount your company will match. You can surely save more, but if you save less, you'll be leaving free money on the table.

Most companies also offer various medical reimbursement plans. There aren't too many places that provide a pension anymore—they've mostly been replaced by 401(k) plans—but if you're at a job that offers a pension and all else is well, you may want to consider staying there long enough to collect it.

If your position involves travel, chances are a per diem is provided. More than likely, you wouldn't have a travel schedule as busy as that of a player in a team sport, but if you travel often enough, those per diems could start to add up. And while you're booking trips, make sure to get your frequent-flyer miles. Those add up, too.

Aside from your job and the above-mentioned benefits,

you can create your own supplementary income stream. The most obvious thing to do is to get a second job. Many people do this and earmark that second income for a specific bill or set of bills, or they may use it to fund their retirement account, or it could even just be their spending money.

There are other reasons to obtain a second job. United Parcel Service (UPS) is the fourth-largest employer in the United States, and as such has a very lucrative benefits program that even part-time employees can take advantage of. They are essentially offering full-time benefits to part-time employees. For this reason, if you have a full-time job with a substandard benefits package, working at a place like UPS may be the perfect second job. Admittedly, companies that offer this kind of package are becoming scarce, but with a little research you should be able to find some company that offers benefits to part-timers.

You can also start your own business on the side. It's a lot easier than people think, because you don't necessarily have to locate and rent office or retail space, then find employees, etc. If you're artistically inclined, you can simply sell your own artwork from home. Create a website to get your name and art out to the public and go from there. Maybe you got the job that you have because of the top-notch résumé

SECRET FROM AN ATHLETE'S PLAYBOOK: *Maintaining a clean reputation and a good image will allow you access to supplemental income streams throughout your professional life.*

you wrote. If you think you can write one for someone else, make that your side business. With the economy the way it has been over the last several years, there are lots of job seekers out there who would be willing to pay for an improved résumé.

Whatever business you take on, you should formalize it once you're making around $5,000 a year for three consecutive years. A lawyer and an accountant can help you do that. Whether it's something small that you operate from your home, or the beginnings of a company that you think will grow into a multimillion-dollar venture, there is money to be made outside of the confines of your 9 to 5.

TIPS

1. Always make the maximum allowable 401(k) contribution.
2. Find income sources other than your job.
3. Hire an attorney to negotiate your contract.
4. Try to save as much money as you can.
5. Stay with a company long enough to obtain a pension.
6. Take advantage of your company's medical reimbursement plan.
7. Once you are making good money on the side, formalize your business.

Let's take a look at two fictitious basketball players, Big Baller Tom and Steady John, to see how they are managing with their incomes. Steady John and Big Baller Tom have each signed three-year, $6 million contracts.

BIG BALLER TOM

Tom has a big personality, and the media loves him. With endorsement deals and summer camp revenue, his total income is significantly greater than Steady John's. Tom's total earnings over the course of three years are outlined below.

Contract:	$6,000,000
Endorsements:	$1,000,000
Basketball Camps:	$100,000
401k: ($41,000 × 3 years)	$123,000
Medical Reimbursements:	$60,000
($20,000 × 3 years)	
Licensing Check:	$75,000
([$35,000−$10,000 NBPA] × 3 years)	
Pension:	$0
(does not apply until 3 years of service)	
Per Diem:	$14,760
($120 per travel day × ~41 days minimum × 3 years)	
Playoff Bonus:	$5,000
(making it to playoffs; 1 year)	

Total:	$7,377,760

STEADY JOHN

Aside from the contract Steady John signed, his other streams of income include endorsements and camp appearances.

Contract:	$6,000,000
Endorsements:	$100,000
Basketball Camps:	$15,000
($5,000 × 3 years)	
401k: ($41,000 × 3 years)	$123,000
Medical Reimbursements:	$60,000
($20,000 × 3 years)	
Licensing Check:	$75,000
($35,000−$10,000 NBPA × 3 years)	
Pension:	$0
(does not apply until 3 years of service)	
Per Diem:	$14,760
($120 per travel day × ~41 days minimum × 3 years)	
Playoff Bonus (making it to playoffs; 1 year)	$5,000
Total	$6,392,760

NBA players have many potential income streams, and so do you. If you manage your income with care, it will offer you a lifetime of economic independence. There is a saying, *It's not what you make, but what you keep.* This might be truer for professional athletes than for any other group, but it is true for you as well.

CHAPTER FOUR

EQUIPMENT

TAMING YOUR WANTS AND FULFILLING YOUR NEEDS

Turn on any television show that features celebrity homes and it's not hard to see what we as a society have come to cherish. It's all about fancy "cribs" and expensive "whips." Now, don't get me wrong. These lifestyle choices are fine if you can afford them. The reality, however, is that most can't afford that stuff. Even a pro athlete whom you may consider to be wealthy may not be able to afford a fleet of high-end cars once he takes a good, hard look at his overall finances.

Overspending by professional athletes shouldn't be a surprise, since we've been brought up in a culture that measures success by the number of extravagant items a person has, from bling to whips to cribs and, in some cases . . . that private jet. The problem is that most athletes don't understand or at least prioritize the difference between wants and needs. Needs are necessities for getting along in life. Wants are things that people desire, but are not critical to continuing on day to day. People need water to survive, but they might want Dom Pérignon. They need clothing and a place to stay, but they might want Tom Ford and a mansion. Pro athletes are a good example here. They have to get to work like everybody else, but a lot of them want to get there in a Bentley that they don't need and can't afford. You, on the other hand, may work right near the subway stop, but take taxis to the job four out of five days. Can you really afford that? How much is that over the course of a month . . . or a year?

In the words of former NFL coach Herman Edwards, "You got champagne taste, but you only got beer money. That's not good!"

Many NBA, NFL, and MLB players come from a modest background, and for most, signing a pro contract is the first time they've had any money—even a small amount. When you haven't had money, any amount can seem like you've been given the keys to Fort Knox.

That's because of what's known as the poverty mentality. Some people focus on what they don't have instead of what they do. It's sort of like viewing the glass as half-empty instead of half-full. Thinking that one can't afford something or that one will never have enough money can lead to one's never actually getting out of poverty. Zig Ziglar, an author and motivational speaker, was among the first to discuss this. He noted that people who make it out of poverty are the ones who are able to view what they do have as positive and therefore are able to make a real plan and work their way up. But the poverty mentality is tough to shake. That's what leads athletes to buy a Bentley with their first paycheck instead of setting up a retirement plan.

The same is true for anyone, no matter what level he or she is on. A high earner can spend more than her $3.5-million-a-year salary can withstand just as easily as a management-level worker can spend more than the $75,000 a year that he gets. So, it goes without saying that a recent college grad making $30,000 can spend more than he has, even when keeping up with the basic necessities takes him right to the edge as it is. The bottom line is, you need to learn what you can afford and stay within your means.

HOUSES

How often do you see players with multiple cars, big luxury mansions, and massive amounts of jewelry? Most of the time, expenses like that are perfectly justifiable and legitimate. Pro athletes work all their lives to get to that point, so they are entitled to reward themselves with something nice. One thing a player usually wants when he first gets money is to buy a house for his mother. Of course, he'll want his own house, too. That's *two* houses right there. And even though players buy these homes with cash, they'll still have to pay the property taxes and for the upkeep of the homes for the rest of their lives. If an athlete is going to buy a house for his mom, he might as well give her enough money to pay the property taxes for the rest of her life, too.

The expenses of a house can be onerous. To put these

expenses in better perspective, here is a list of things that may very well have to be paid for while you own a house . . . or two:

+ Mortgage
+ Water
+ Electricity
+ Waste management
+ Cable
+ Internet
+ Security system

+ Cleaning service
+ Lawn services
+ Upkeep
+ Property tax
+ Pool services
+ Pest control
+ Telephone

Also, homes can be a liability rather than an asset. A home generally causes you to take out a loan that, in all honesty, you probably can't afford. Houses, cars, and jewelry are all liabilities, because their value decreases over time. Therefore, you are losing money in the long run. Stocks, bonds, mutual funds, and even artwork are examples of assets that increase in value, thus raising your net worth.

No one is saying that you shouldn't own a house. In fact, owning a house or a condo is preferable to paying rent because of tax deductions available to home owners. For instance, the interest on a home owner's mortgage loan is tax-deductible. So is the property tax, believe it or not. Buying a home is investing in the real estate market, which can potentially yield some return on investment. But sometimes, depending on the state of the housing market and where your house is located, you might have to wait a long time for that return. Let's say you own a house in San Francisco or Washington,

D.C. Those are cities where property values continually rise, so you're going to get a positive return on your investment. On the other hand, though the homes in cities like Philadelphia and Orlando don't necessarily appreciate in value, they're lower-priced, making it easier for first-time buyers to enter the world of home ownership.

Another advantage to owning a home is that in the top one hundred markets in the United States, it's about 35 percent cheaper to buy a house than it is to rent.

When buying a house, you should make sure that the size and cost of your house is aligned with your income. For example, even if an athlete buys a house for $3 million and is fortunate enough to be able to pay it off, depending on the state he lives in, his property tax could be as much as $30,000 a year. Will he make enough money in retirement to cover that and all the other needs a house like that would require?

You can scale that down, and a $1 million house could have taxes upward of $10,000 a year and a $300,000 house could require you to pay $3,000 every year. On top of all of your other expenses, can you afford an additional $3,000 every year?

Losing your home, whether it's due to foreclosure or being unable to keep up with the taxes, can be a very emotional event for anyone who's invested time and money into obtaining and maintaining the property. Not only that, but if this is your primary residence, there will be an emotional attachment as well, and it's anybody's guess as to how that might play itself out.

Several years after Robert Swift left the NBA, his house

in Washington State was foreclosed on. He refused to leave and stayed there with his girlfriend even after another couple purchased the home from the bank. He finally got out before the sheriff was called, but the condition he left the house in reveals a person with serious emotional issues and/or someone who really didn't want to leave his home. The new owners found punched-out walls, framed photos, autographs, and a box of letters—scholarship offers, from college programs like UCLA, Kentucky, and Kansas, addressed to Swift dating back to his high school days. There was also a makeshift gun range in the basement, complete with bullet holes and slugs in the beams of the house. Multiple guns were strewn throughout the house as well.

Leaving a home, even when it's been foreclosed on, doesn't usually involve that kind of drama; but, as we've learned from stories like Chris Tucker's home going into foreclosure and MC Hammer's losing his Oakland Hills compound, tales of former greats falling from riches to rags are all too common.

CLOTHING

Athletes spend money on clothes. Clothing was a non-issue in the NBA for a long time; but in 2005, when the owners put it on the table during the renewal of the collective bargaining agreement, it moved front and center, and it became a national headline when the NBA's CBA included a dress code. There was a little resistance at first, but since then, players have come to think of themselves as fashion icons.

They purchase the most expensive designer clothes, generally from tailors who show up at the hotel while the team is on the road. Some players simply like to look good and pay anywhere from $1,500 to $3,000 for a suit. I know several players who have bought as many as a hundred of those $3,000 suits at one time. I imagine some sort of discount was worked out, but I know those suits were still not cheap.

Though it's nowhere near what the NBA guys are paying, a place like Men's Wearhouse can be pretty expensive, too—its suits for the most part run in the $500 to $800 range. However, for most of you just starting out, Burlington Coat Factory would be a good bet. Designer suits there can go for under $200. If the guys buying suits in the hotel on the road were smart, they'd go to Burlington Coat Factory, too.

All of us should set a wardrobe budget and stick with it. Buying too many clothes is a luxury that can drain your income. A lot of players also have personal shoppers, which can cost anywhere from $10,000 to $30,000 a year on top of the cost of the clothes. And remember: Clothes go out of style every year and can rarely be resold.

Due to the dress code, along with the need for special exercise attire, a portion of NBA players' clothing expenses can be tax-deductible (which they should be sure to bring up with their accountants).

Lots of people who are not necessarily in the public eye are very concerned about their daily wardrobe, and some may even be addicted to shopping. While looking good is important no matter what you do on a daily basis, there is no need to go out of your budget just to keep from having to walk the streets naked. You need only a few good outfits to get you by.

CARS

A car purchase is one the most significant expenses you will face. I can't tell you how many times I've seen teammates run out and buy the most expensive car they can, like a Bentley, just to maintain an image. The worst part is that, most of the time, they end up not even liking the car. Bentleys are flimsy, and for a big, young dude running the streets after practice, this is no good. I know two players who bought their Bentleys at the same time. Six months later, one had sold his, complaining among other things that the cup holders were unusable, and the other just kept his in the garage and never drove it. This is an example of just blowing money for no reason. That kind of car is nothing but a big burden. Expensive to gas up. Expensive to maintain. Expensive to insure.

When I first entered the league in 1997, I bought a Toyota 4Runner as my first car. I was so excited to be in a financial position to buy a car outright. It was a great moment for me. I had done the research—it was strong, had good resale value, and was going to last me a long time. After growing up with a donkey for transportation, the idea of buying a car, let alone a brand-new one, signified my huge step up in many ways.

I was extremely proud of my car. But when my teammates showed up to practice in their Mercedes, BMWs, Escalades, and Rolls-Royces, they laughed at my 4Runner! They even tried to clown me by asking if it was my car while trying to keep from busting out laughing. I couldn't figure out what was wrong with buying a car I could afford, especially one that was great for resale. I ignored them.

I upgraded to a Lincoln Navigator several years and a couple of contracts later, when I could afford it. I keep it in California; my other car, a Cadillac Escalade that I bought secondhand, is in Florida. Of course, I bought the Escalade used, but everybody thinks it's new. Interestingly enough, the Escalade and the Navigator both spend more time in the repair shop than my Toyota ever did.

Most people purchase their first vehicle on credit. I knew players who had as many as six cars—and not inexpensive ones, either. Those guys end up paying much more for the car when they buy on credit and pay interest on the loan. When you have the money, it doesn't make financial sense to not pay for a car outright.

Professional athletes love cars, but there are some serious drawbacks, even when paid for up front. The minute a car drives off the lot, it depreciates in value. All cars depreciate in value over time, yet players will still buy four, five, even *six* cars. You can drive only one car at a time. How many cars do you really need? When guys are drooling at the dealership, they seem to forget that they also have to pay insurance for all those cars. And then there's the cost of *maintaining* them all— and exotic cars are expensive to maintain. All a fleet of exotic cars does is unnecessarily drain your money and resources.

As far as I'm concerned, there is nothing wrong with having two cars, or even three, if the price is reasonable—and especially if the athlete has a family. But when athletes start purchasing three and four luxury cars, they might as well cut a hole in their pocket and let the money fall out. As a matter of fact, the hole-in-the-pocket thing might be less expensive.

For most of us, the car payment is our second-largest bill after the rent or mortgage. There is nothing wrong with going with a cheaper make of car than you had your heart set on. In this day and age, there is no such thing as a bad car. In other words, a brand-new Acura is not going to leave you stranded on the side of the road, but neither is a brand-new Hyundai.

JEWELRY

A lot of pro athletes feel they haven't "made it" until they purchase the most expensive jewelry in the store. A $75,000 watch . . . $25,000 bracelet . . . $50,000 necklace. That's $150,000 in jewelry right off the bat. Granted, jewelry is not the worst thing in the world, because buyers can sometimes reinvest it—but when pros spend $150,000 on "bling," that money's not earning *anything* at the moment. Additionally, athletes' jewelry is often personalized, and as a result, not even their biggest fan would want to purchase it (and even if their biggest fan did want it, chances are he wouldn't be able to afford it). Personalized jewelry has limited resale value. Athletes can sell their jewelry on a piecemeal basis, but it would still be for a much lower price than what they originally paid.

Carefully selected jewelry is not a horrible investment,

but if done so at the expense of investing in one's stock port-folio or retirement account, the opportunity lost could lead to dire consequences. Sometimes, when a player walks into a jewelry store, he could wind up buying a necklace for three or four times its actual value because he has no knowledge of how much that chain is really worth. You should have the right people around you not only to provide the knowledge necessary to make informed decisions about purchasing jew-elry but sometimes to actually negotiate for you.

Wearing expensive jewelry, especially on easily visible areas of their bodies, also makes athletes vulnerable to theft. In 2002, while playing for the New Jersey Nets, Chris Childs was in Manhattan walking from P. Diddy's restaurant, Jus-tin's, to his nearby Mercedes-Benz, when he was approached and robbed at gunpoint. The robber got away with $30,000 in jewelry and cash.

Also in Manhattan, in 2000, Brooklyn native Stephon Marbury was sitting in his Bentley when two men ap-proached the car. Neither had a weapon, but one reached in the car and snatched the $150,000 chain off Stephon's neck.

Antoine Walker was robbed not once but twice. In 2000, he was part of a group of people robbed at gunpoint. Among the things the thieves made off with were his $55,000 watch and $3,000 in cash. Later, in 2007, Walker was the victim of a home invasion when gunmen broke in, tied him up with duct tape, then went through the house and stole $200,000 in valuables.

Admittedly, most of the young players coming up now don't wear so much jewelry—that was more of a thing with the last generation. But expensive watches, glasses, electronics, and so on litter today's locker rooms, and all of the rules for jewelry should still apply.

TIPS

1. Understand the difference between wants and needs.
2. There is a time and a place to wear expensive jewelry. Protect your assets and wear them only when going to high-end functions, like charity galas or weddings.
3. When shopping, take an expert who knows about jewelry and is a capable market researcher.
4. Buy a safe to store your jewelry, or use a security box at a bank.
5. Consider tax breaks for clothing expenses related to your career.
6. Resist the temptation to live above your means. Don't try to keep up with the Joneses . . . or the Bryants, Durants, and Jameses. Do what is best for you.
7. Set a wardrobe budget a year in advance.

Professional athletes have worked their entire lives to get to this level, and there's nothing wrong with enjoying life and splurging a little. Getting a nice car or buying a home is a luxury athletes should enjoy. Dressing up nicely and wearing a little bling is okay as well—but don't overindulge. You *have* to put money away so that when your career is over, your lifestyle doesn't come to a screeching halt. You don't want to end up on an episode of *Pawn Stars,* selling your championship ring and your custom jewelry. That would make for a pathetic story line: the gladiator who has battled in the arena his entire life—only to lose it all in the end.

THE PLAYERS

BIG BALLER TOM

Big Baller Tom opted for a million-dollar house for himself and a half-million-dollar house for his mother. From purchasing time slots on private jets to spending $100,000 on clothes, Tom, it's safe to say, made some questionable financial decisions that will cost him later.

Remaining Income:	$7,377,760

LIFESTYLE EXPENSES

House:	−$1,000,000
Mom's house:	−$500,000
Jewelry:	−$200,000
Car 1:	−$100,000
Car 2:	−$150,000
Clothing:	−$100,000
Plane (25 hours):	−$160,000
Total Lifestyle Expenses:	−$2,210,000

Income After Lifestyle Expenses:	$5,167,760

STEADY JOHN

Steady John opted for an apartment instead of a house and decided to buy one car outright. He spent more than he wanted to on clothes but decided it would help his endorsement potential.

Remaining Income:	$6,392,760

LIFESTYLE EXPENSES

Apartment:	−$70,000
Jewelry:	−$10,000
Car:	−$40,000
Clothing:	−$29,000
Plane:	−$0
Total Lifestyle Expenses:	$149,000

Income After Lifestyle Expenses:	$6,243,760

CHAPTER FIVE

TOO MANY BALLS IN THE AIR

RECREATIONAL SPENDING

In October 2000, the Philadelphia 76ers and Toronto Raptors were warming up before a meaningless preseason game. Both teams were still wearing their warm-ups and running layup lines as the crowd was filing into the arena when the Raptors' Charles Oakley crossed over to the Sixers end of the court and started yelling at one of their players. No one really knew what was going on, but then Oakley approached and slapped power forward Tyrone Hill. A scuffle started but was quickly broken up by the other players. Both Oakley and Hill were ejected before the game even started.

A few months later, during the regular season, the two teams met again, this time in Philadelphia. During the warm-ups on this night, Oakley hurled several basketballs at Hill, hitting him in the head with one. Oak was fined $10,000 and suspended for one game because of the incident. No one could figure out what their beef was, but it was later revealed that Hill had lost $54,000 to Oakley in a dice game. Tyrone wasn't paying up, so Oakley took matters into his own hands. In May 2001, the two teams met in the playoffs, and when the Raptors came to Philadelphia for Game Five of the series, Hill went to the Raptors' team hotel and paid Oakley the money.

The worst-kept secret in America is that pro athletes, with all that money, have an affinity for gambling. For example, John Daly reportedly bet ridiculous amounts of money on golf. In his book *John Daly: My Life in and out of the Rough*, he claims that he lost between $50 and $60 million in a twelve-year period of serious gambling. He also tells a story about earning $750,000 at a World Golf Championship in San Francisco when he lost in a playoff to Tiger Woods. Instead of going home, he drove to Las Vegas, and claims to have lost $1.65 million in five hours, mostly playing $5,000 slot machines.

Similarly, Charles Barkley claims he's lost over $10 million at casinos. Chuck admitted recently that gambling "is a problem for me. My agent has really worked with me to try to get it where I can go and gamble and have fun. That's easier said than done. Do I have a gambling problem? Yeah, I do have a gambling problem but I don't consider it a problem because I can afford to gamble. It's just a stupid habit that I've got to get under control, because it's just not a good thing to be broke after all of these years."

It seems to me that Chuck *can't* afford to lose that money. I understand that he has a lot of money, but no matter how much you have, $10 million is a lot to lose recreationally. There has got to be a cheaper hobby. Barkley and Daly are examples of rich athletes letting their gambling get out of hand. Gambling is essentially recreational spending, and while it can be figured into your budget, it should be a lot less than the amount of money these guys are burning.

For those who are not rich athletes, recreational spending in a budget looks much different. Goods and services that a nine-to-fiver would consider recreational spending, such as eating out, gym memberships, sports equipment, audiovisual equipment, books, and travel are things that pro athletes can afford, and afford to overindulge in at that. So addictive gambling is the only kind of recreational spending athletes indulge in that they can feel right away, whereas you may notice the difference in your account after a night out at a restaurant.

Each year, both the NBA and NFL offer seminars that teach young players about the perils of gambling. But probably because professional sports organizations worry about the sanctity and purity of the game, no one is really talking about the negative effect gambling has on individual players and their financial stability.

It's very rare for athletes to actually bet on their own games, but they are notorious for wanting to bet on themselves in other ways. During NBA practices, players bet on sinking a half-court shot, on making a behind-the-basket shot, on sitting on the bench and nailing a three, or on winning a game of H-O-R-S-E. They love betting on themselves to win and think the more money they bet, the greater confidence they're displaying in themselves. Gambling is a way for them to prove their own greatness—not just in practice but in the game of life.

Gambling has seeped its way into the mainstream's perception of athletes. Remember the famous McDonald's commercial with Michael Jordan playing a "friendly" game of H-O-R-S-E with Larry Bird? This campaign worked, in part, because it spoke to the inherently competitive nature of athletes. There's a rumor making its way through the league that Michael Jordan used to carry around a' briefcase with $5 million in cash for gambling. Whether this story is true or not, it falls in line with the characteristics of a compulsive gambler. And let's not forget, Michael Jordan is the man who, one night, wouldn't let his roommate go to sleep until he was able to beat him at a video game. He also wouldn't stop betting on shots with his Washington Wizards teammate Richard "Rip" Hamilton one day after a shootaround. MJ made the entire team wait on the bus while he tried to win his money back from Rip.

But it was two other Wizards who took gambling beef among athletes to a new level. In 2009, Gilbert Arenas and Javaris Crittendon were gambling on the team's flight from Phoenix back to Washington, D.C. The friendly game turned ugly when one of them apparently wouldn't pay the other, and they nearly came to blows. Their argument continued as they got off the plane, with both men vowing to "handle it" the next day. They weren't kidding. The next day, their argument picked right up in the locker room, to which both of them had brought guns. They apparently weren't afraid to use them, for each pulled his out and threatened the other.

They both ended up suspended for the rest of the season without pay, as it is in violation of the CBA to bring guns to any NBA facility or when conducting any NBA business. Obviously, they knew that they shouldn't have guns in the locker room, but the argument over a gambling dispute got both of them so upset that they disregarded the union contract—which ended up costing them a lot of money, in addition to the hit to their reputations.

Gambling can become a major wealth-destroyer for pro athletes, who often gamble at such a high level that it's not uncommon to see $20,000 in chips leave their hands at a casino table. Because they have so much money at their disposal, it's very easy for this to become an addiction or at least a serious problem. Gambling athletes tend to think that whatever they lose they can make back with their next paycheck. Even worse, while athletes' guaranteed income ends after they retire, their gambling addiction often doesn't, and too late they may realize that having the mentality that gambling can demonstrate one's self-worth is a distorted reality that'll run a bank account dry.

Meanwhile, a new flat-screen TV and sound bar for your bedroom could run *your* bank account dry, but at least you're not looking at the TV as a measure of self-worth . . . hopefully.

Serious issues with gambling can be divided into two categories. The first is a Gambling Addiction, also known as Compulsive Gambling. The second is a Gambling Problem. NBA players can occupy either category.

Addicted gamblers wouldn't be able to relate to Kenny Rogers's lyrics from "The Gambler," because the very nature of this addiction prevents them from folding, holding, or walking away, let alone running. Gambling addiction is a serious mental disorder, and athletes afflicted with it need to seek out professional help right away, because even if they know their behavior is destructive to themselves and their family and friends, they can't stop. No matter what the emotional or financial consequences of their behavior may be, they'll still drive down to Atlantic City for a quick fix.

Problem gamblers, on the other hand, have issues with gambling, but their behavior is not totally out of control. Still, it may be disruptive to their lives, as gambling can strain relationships and interfere with responsibilities at home and on the team. While not as severe an issue as compulsive gambling, problem gambling often has a serious negative impact on finances as well. Problem gamblers can lose hundreds of thousands of dollars in a single year—making financial catastrophe the most significant issue facing both compulsive and problem gamblers.

There are a number of guys who don't see gambling as a problem, but there is always concern. "You can't beat the casino," said Charles Barkley about his gambling habit. "You might win a lot of money from them, but in the long run they are going to win more money from you, and I've got to get to a point where I don't gamble for as much."

A few years back, I went down to the Bahamas with a group for a players' union conference. One evening after our meetings were over for the day, I stood and watched one of my fellow union members sit down at a casino table and buy in for $125,000. Gambling at this level can put you right in the poorhouse . . . or the big house.

Antoine Walker, a three-time All-Star who played twelve seasons in the NBA, with Boston, Dallas, Atlanta, Miami, and Minnesota, was arrested in 2009 and charged with three felony counts of passing checks with insufficient funds to three Las Vegas casinos. Gambling debts in Nevada are handled as bad-check cases. Walker, who won championships with the Heat in 2006 and at the University of Kentucky in 1996, let his gambling get out of control and was arrested at Harrah's in South Lake Tahoe. Two years later, he was still dealing with it, as he was sentenced to five years of probation and ordered to pay more than $770,050 in gambling debts to the three casinos.

TIPS

1. If you're not a gambler, don't start.
2. Find out if you fall into the category of addictive or problem gambling. There is a website (www.help guide.org) that helps you make an assessment.
3. If you choose to gamble socially, you should keep track of how much you win and lose, so that at the end of six months, you can see how much you've spent.
4. You should try to limit gambling to social settings so it doesn't grow into a serious issue.

5. You should only play games that you're familiar with.
6. Always have a plan. Before you get to Vegas, set aside some gambling money that you can afford to part with.
7. Only spend what you can afford.

While an athlete's problem could be with gambling, your issue could be with shopping excessively, purchasing items on credit cards, and going into debt. This habit could be as crippling to your budget as gambling can be to an athlete's. My point is that it is important to control recreational spending. Some money abusers spend too much money on drugs, tobacco, or alcohol. Another bad habit could be an addiction to shoes.

Athletes gamble for many reasons, including believing that they can't lose and asserting their confidence. Some also see gambling as a way to replicate that adrenaline rush they feel when they're on the court. Gambling can provide a temporary relief for some, but it can also come with horrible consequences, putting the gambler in emotional and financial quicksand. On the same note, you should not spend beyond your money on frivolous or unnecessary purchases. Do you really need that new TV? Wouldn't it make more

SECRET FROM THE LOCKER ROOM: *Exercising discipline reaps great rewards.*

sense to go grocery shopping for the week instead of eating out every night?

THE PLAYERS

Many players like to gamble, and these guys are no exceptions.

BIG BALLER TOM

Big Baller Tom is blowing money at the casino with reckless abandon. He really needs to be careful, because gambling is one sure way to lose your money without understanding where it went.

Remaining Income:	$5,167,760
Gambling losses:	−$100,000
Food:	−$5,000
Hotel rooms:	−$5,000
Strip clubs:	−$5,000
Total Gambling Expense:	−$115,000
Income After Gambling Expenses:	$5,052,760

STEADY JOHN

Steady John went to Las Vegas a few times but spent only $10,000. He likes the food there more than the gambling.

Remaining Income:	$6,243,760
Gambling losses:	−$10,000
Food:	−$5,000
Hotel rooms:	−$5,000
Total loss:	$20,000

Income After Gambling Expenses:	$6,223,760

CHAPTER SIX

PAYING TO PLAY

DEALING WITH TAXES

The vocal and charismatic Warren Sapp was the leader of the Tampa Bay Buccaneers defense in 2002 when the team won its only Super Bowl. Over the course of his NFL career, which stretched from 1996 to 2007, he signed three different contracts. The first was for $4.4 million, the second was for $36.05 million, and the third was for $36.46 million. Five years after his retirement from football, he filed for bankruptcy, listing more than $6.7 million in debts.

The Chapter 7 bankruptcy filing included among his assets 240 pairs of Air Jordans, some of which he later had to auction off to pay back child support. Among his debts, most of which were business-related rather than personal debts, was $90,685 to National Car Rental; $822,805 to PNC Bank, for which the bank had been garnishing $33,333 out of Sapp's $45,000 monthly paycheck from NFL Network; and $876,000 in alimony and child support to his ex-wife.

There were also several tax bills. There was the $68,738 in property taxes he had to pay on his mansion in Windermere, Florida, where his ex-wife was living while he lived in a Miami condo. He owed $89,775 from his 2010 income taxes. The IRS was also looking for $853,003 from Sapp's 2006 earnings.

In September 2012, a judge ruled that Sapp had gotten his financials back in order and dismissed the case. Although most of his debts were wiped away at that point, the tax bills were not. Bankruptcy does not protect you from paying taxes, so the $68,738 property tax and the $89,775 and $853,003 income tax bills were still due.

In 2013, Americans paid a combined $2.5 trillion in federal taxes. More than $3 billion of that was paid by NBA, MLB, and NFL players. That's a lot of money from a workforce of about three thousand people. Players from those three sports earned nearly $9 billion that year and are generally taxed at the highest rate of more than 39 percent. The average football, baseball, or basketball player owes around $1 million in federal taxes each year. The key word here is "owes," because as we know, not everyone chooses to pay. But eventually the IRS catches up.

Nothing is certain except death and taxes. Surely you've heard that saying before. Whether it was some character on TV, a teacher, or one of your parents who first said it in your presence, that person was right. It was actually written by Ben Franklin in a 1789 letter explaining why the Constitution should be made permanent. Franklin, who discovered electricity, formed the first library in America, and created the nation's first hospital, clearly understood the concept of taxes, because in the more than 225 years since he wrote that, Americans have been paying them, and it doesn't really look like there is an end in sight.

To protect your money, I suggest you find a good CPA or tax preparer. Pay your taxes on time with his assistance and you'll be in the best position to hold on to as much of your pretax money as possible. Throughout the course of the year, keep your CPA in the loop by informing him of all your sources of income. This will allow him to create a good tax payment plan. It is legal to aggressively seek deductions, and many are available. What is not legal is to avoid paying the taxes that you *do* owe. People who think they can get away with not paying their taxes inevitably find themselves in deep financial trouble. No matter how far a person runs, the government will always catch up.

DEATH AND TAXES

Recently, the IRS announced that it will auction off the remainder of former New York Met Darryl Strawberry's salary to pay off $543,000 he owes in tax arrears from 1989, 1990, 2003, and 2004. When Strawberry signed a $7.1 million contract with the Mets in 1985, $700,000 of it was put into an annuity with a 5.1 percent annual interest. The annuity, which is what is being auctioned off, will pay out approximately $1.3 million over nineteen years. Buying the annuity was a smart move on Strawberry's part, because twenty years after he signed his contract with the Mets he is still getting paid, and would have for the next nineteen years had he not gotten into trouble with the IRS.

As a high-income earner, you can work out a plan that pays off all tax debts at the end of the year, but that's not really the smartest thing to do. You don't know how big that bill is going to be at the end of the year, and no matter how much it is, you won't be happy about cutting a check for that entire lump sum.

If you're working for a company, you may want to have additional money taken from your paycheck every week. When filling out your W–2 form, you can simply write in the amount of any additional money you want the government to withhold and apply it to your taxes at the end of the year. Doing it this way ensures that you will have paid your tax requirement and that you may even get a refund. You can also claim exemptions when you file your taxes in order to lower the amount you have to pay. Exemptions are essentially items that the government has determined are not taxable and that therefore will lower the amount of taxable income you have. For instance, if you purchase municipal bonds, the interest on those bonds is tax-exempt, so you don't have to pay federal income taxes on it.

Of course, you may not have a problem with waiting until the end of the year to pay your tax liabilities, or maybe you're okay with paying exactly what your CPA estimates you'll owe—but that's how you can end up not paying enough, and in trouble with the IRS.

To be clear, if you're working at a job and are paid with a payroll check, then all of your income taxes are taken out before you even get paid. If that job is your only income, then you probably don't have much to worry about. Your employer takes out the federal, state, and local taxes. It is structured so that, in most cases, you are overpaying throughout the course of the year. This is where your refund comes from—that overpayment. And this is why it is so important for you to file. The National Foundation for Credit Counseling conducted an online poll and found that the majority of Americans overpay on taxes and that this is the primary way that they are able to save money. When people get their tax refund, they usually catch up on bills. But while many pay off debts with their tax refunds, others use the money to take vacations or buy new furniture or even make a down payment on a car.

If you have various streams of income in addition to your job, like from your own business, most likely that money is coming in untaxed. When you receive untaxed income, you should put half of it away to pay the tax on it later. Chances are the taxes on that money won't equal 50 percent, but that is the amount tax experts have agreed you should put aside.

Whether by placing money into an account to hold for the IRS or by claiming various exemptions on your income tax filing, you and your CPA need to make a plan. You don't want to make any mistakes, because it's not uncommon for the IRS to send someone a bill for $1.6 million out of the $3.4 million he earned that year. It's also not uncommon for the IRS to send out a bill for $22,000 of the $45,000 someone earned in a given year. If you do receive a large tax bill that you can't pay, you should hire a CPA right away to represent you in your dealings with the IRS. The CPA will offer advice to you and talk to the IRS on your behalf. You will have to give the CPA limited power of attorney for this.

Former New York Giants linebacker Lawrence Taylor failed to claim all of his income on his 1990 federal tax return. Under an agreement with prosecutors in 2000, Taylor pleaded guilty to shorting the Internal Revenue Service $48,000. The Hall of Famer was ordered to pay the back taxes plus a $10,000 fine. He was also sentenced to three months of house arrest, five years of probation, and five hundred hours of community service. The IRS does not play!

I see athletes get in trouble for tax evasion all the time, and when I do, I don't blame them—I blame the CPA. Anyone earning the kind of money that a professional athlete pulls in is not doing his own taxes; he hires a CPA so that he doesn't run into problems. That's why it is necessary to take your time to find a good CPA. Talk to other people at your job, the manager at your bank, or any other trusted advisers you have about whom they use. Then, don't take their word for it—do some additional research on your own. If the tax preparer has been audited several times, seek services elsewhere. Even if he's coming out of the audits okay, it means that the government is watching him for some reason. This person will be filling one of the most important roles in your life from here on out, so it's crucial to have a good and honest relationship, because you do *not* want the IRS knocking on your door.

"I got audited by the IRS three times," recalls former NBA center Marc Jackson. "The reason why that happened was because the IRS didn't think a big guy like me was showing horses. It wasn't the money I made in the NBA. They just didn't believe that I could spend $30,000 on a horse farm or a ranch.

"I told them they could come to my ranch and see. They did. Three times. They even snuck in there at night. Each time I got audited, they actually wound up owing *me* money. All three times, they audited me because they didn't believe that I had a cattle ranch. If I didn't have a solid accountant, the outcome could have been much different."

Jackson makes a great argument for paying taxes on time and for being an active participant in the process. Showing horses allowed him $30,000 in deductions, and the IRS wanted to confirm it.

DEDUCTIONS

Your taxes are impacted by the amount of deductions, or "write-offs," that you claim. A write-off is a legitimate expense that you can subtract from your taxable income. Let's say you earned $40,000 for the year. The government would tax that amount in full. But if you contributed $3,500 to charity over the course of the year, your income would be adjusted to

$36,500, and the IRS would tax you for that amount, so that you'd pay less than if you had not given to the charity.

Everyone who pays taxes in the United States gets a standard deduction, and it's only when you exceed that deduction that itemizing benefits you. The amount of the standard deduction changes every year, so checking with your tax adviser or even a human resources administrator at your job is important here. If you own a home, there are several tax deductions you can get, such as your mortgage interest; certain closing costs on a newly purchased home, whether they were paid by you or the seller; and the property tax on your home. Sport is a specialized profession to which certain specific deductions are applicable. For the rest of you, as long as you aren't supported by your parents and claimed by them on their taxes, you can deduct items like moving expenses to relocate for a job; student loan interest, even if paid by Mom and Dad; and job-hunting costs, including transportation and lodging if your search took you out of town. Contributions to your 401(k) are also tax-deductible.

There are also many purchases that can be itemized. For pro athletes, the costs of athletic clothes, gym memberships, and even fees for personal nutritionists could be used as deductions. For a graphic designer, art supplies, computer software, or food and drinks at an art exhibit could all be itemized. Work boots, warm clothes, and other protective gear are among the clothing and shoes that can be deducted by construction workers, garbage collectors, postal carriers, or anyone else who works outdoors.

The quickest way to risk emptying your bank account, going to jail, or both is by not paying your taxes. The IRS doesn't care who you are or what you do; it wants the money that it is legally owed. And you'd better watch out, because the IRS *will* hold you upside down by your ankles and shake until every cent you owe drops out.

Pro athletes having run-ins with the IRS are not a new phenomenon. Boxer Joe Louis was a well-mannered and likable heavyweight champion back in the 1940s. He donated money to the government after the attacks on Pearl Harbor and provided entertainment and uniforms to thousands of army troops. But when there was a change in the tax code that he was unaware of, he ended up owing the IRS a lot of money. Ultimately, he had to come out of retirement and fight again to help pay off his tax debts. At the time of his death, he hadn't yet paid off the government.

The IRS has the legal right to take anyone's most prized, personal, or precious possessions and sell them to pay off a debt. Pete Rose, who has more hits than anyone else who has ever played Major League Baseball, is probably best known for being banned from the sport for betting on games. Aside from that, he was fined $50,000 and ordered to do a thousand hours of community service for not reporting income from special appearances and autographs. When he was found guilty again in 2003 of not paying taxes, he had to pay $154,000 and sell his condo in Los Angeles. The best defense for high-income earners, or anyone, is to pay their taxes on time and never fall behind.

MANDATORY TAXES

The two taxes that just about everyone has to pay are federal and state. Athletes, however, are also forced to deal with what is unofficially known as the Jock Tax.

Most Americans are required to pay federal tax; however, the United States has a progressive tax system, meaning that the more money someone makes, the more taxes he will pay on it. For pro athletes, the federal tax rate is around 35 percent.

State tax is a different story, though. This has to be paid to whichever state you have declared as your primary residence. Each state takes a different percentage rate; because of that, athletes should give serious thought to where they declare residency.

States like Florida, Texas, and Nevada are desirable for athletes and other high earners because they have no state income tax. There are some basic ways to become a resident of these states, such as registering a car, obtaining a driver's license, registering to vote, or becoming affiliated with a local organization like a church, synagogue, mosque, town watch, volunteer fire department, or any other community-based organization. Conversely, states such as California and New York have income tax rates of more than 10 percent. No one wants to pay the state ten cents out of every dollar earned if there's a way to pay less.

Before deciding where you want to claim residency, you should consider things beyond just the tax incentive. If you're from Washington State and your entire family lives there, maybe living in Florida is not the best thing for you, despite its not having a state tax. For some people, living in a decent school district would outweigh having to pay Indiana's 3 percent tax. Former NBA player Jeff Foster, who spent his entire career with the Indiana Pacers before retiring in 2012, made the decision to move from his home state of Texas to Indiana.

"I'm originally from Texas, which has no state tax," said Foster. "Toward the end of my career, I claimed Indiana because I was there year-round. In Indiana, there's a three percent state tax. But with the games we'd play away, there were compensation laws [that] would knock the taxes down to one and a half percent. It wasn't Texas at the end of the day, but it was close enough."

The Jock Tax is something that average Americans need not worry about unless they have a high-profile career that involves extensive traveling such as a pro athlete or rock star. The name is a reference to the requirement that all professional athletes pay state income tax to every state they played in during the previous year. In other words, if you play a game in New York, you have to pay New York State taxes for the money you made that night. Some cities require you to pay taxes to them as well. The Jock Tax ensures that all MLB, NFL, NBA, and National Hockey League (NHL) players must file taxes in every state they play in, as well as city-level taxes in several of them. Some jurisdictions will even break down the total salary to include *practices* and then tax for those if they took place in their city.

A lot of athletes believe they are targets of the IRS because they're wealthy. They object to the so-called Jock Tax on the grounds that it is unfair to tax them as though they were residents of a city where they have no extended dealings. "I don't send my kids to school in that city and I don't benefit from that city's resources, so I shouldn't have to pay taxes there" is a common attitude. Some even go so far as to call it "taxation without representation." But don't hold your breath waiting for another Boston Tea Party over this one.

It should be noted that ordinary business travelers don't have to pay a Jock Tax, but members of an NBA team's support staff *do*. I'm referring to people from the public relations department, team trainers, and some marketing people. This is extremely unfair, because a lot of these employees make a salary in the $60,000 or even $40,000 range.

Despite the vast amount of money we make, many current and former NBA players have significant tax issues. In 2009, Rick Mahorn filed for bankruptcy, despite having made around $7 million during his career. The reason for his financial woes was a combination of bad investments, the declining value of his home in Detroit, and the fact that he owed more than $200,000 to the IRS.

Dennis Rodman, a Hall of Fame basketball player with five championship rings, amassed great wealth during his career, yet is paying off nearly $350,000 in back taxes.

Athletes from all sports often neglect to pay their taxes on time. The Associated Press reported in August 2012 that baseball great Jose Canseco, who hit 462 home runs during his sixteen-year career, had filed for Chapter 7 bankruptcy in Nevada. The court document lists $21,000 in assets and $1.7 million in liabilities, including a $500,000 debt owed to the Internal Revenue Service.

Then there's Iron Mike Tyson, who, during the course of his boxing career, made more than $400 million and lived in an extravagant mansion, complete with luxury cars and exotic tigers. He filed for Chapter 11 bankruptcy in 2003, citing debts that included $9 million for his divorce settlement and more than $13 million in back taxes.

When you take shortcuts with regard to taxes, it becomes increasingly difficult to catch up. But even worse is that the IRS will charge you interest for unpaid taxes. So, if you underpaid your taxes two years ago, the feds will want their money plus two years of interest.

This may sound a little extreme, but if it comes down to eating or paying taxes, pay first and eat later. When you receive any money outside your regular paycheck, do what I do and split it in half—half for me, half for Uncle Sam. As far as I'm concerned, it's better to be getting money back from the government than it is to owe anything. If I allocate half my untaxed income to my taxes, I'll get a refund every time. Who needs the stress and the headache?

I know that some tax people don't want you to give the government more than it asks for. They would rather you hold it in a high-interest account that is easy to liquidate and take it out when it's time to pay, as opposed to giving the government an interest-free loan. This may be a good option for highly disciplined savers, but for the rest of us, it is better to play it safe. And what can be safer than overpaying your taxes and getting a refund?

For high earners, overpaying *is* a good idea. The stakes are much higher for coming up short at the end of the year for someone who has a great deal of money. An NFL player *is* going to have enough money to overpay on taxes and still keep the cable on. A high earner should get a refund check from Uncle Sam every year and put it directly into the bank.

Professional athletes are not the only people who get in trouble for not paying taxes. Other high-income earners, such as actors and singers, do as well. Consider this: In the 1990s, country music singer Willie Nelson owed $16.7 million in back taxes, penalties, and interest. When he couldn't pay the money, the IRS froze his bank accounts and auctioned off his personal belongings in order to satisfy the bill. It claimed that from 1978 to 1982, he failed to pay $6.5 million in income taxes. Add on $10.2 million in penalties and interest, and that's a hefty sum. Fortunately for Nelson, several of his fans bought his possessions from the estate sale (and later returned them to him).

Nicolas Cage, who has appeared in more than seventy movies, including starring roles in *8MM, Con Air, Face/Off,* and *National Treasure,* owed the federal government $13 million that he "forgot" to pay. He blamed his business manager as he wrote a check to the federal government for more than $6 million to pay down the debt.

Chris Tucker, who played Smokey in the movie *Friday* and whose comedy kept the *Rush Hour* movie franchise moving, also got in trouble for shorting Uncle Sam. Despite being the highest-paid actor in Hollywood back in 2006 when he signed a $25 million deal to make *Rush Hour 3*, Tucker reportedly owed $12 million in taxes because he didn't pay for several years, including 2001, 2002, 2004, 2005, 2006, and 2007. The bank foreclosed on his $6 million Florida home in 2007.

Stephen Baldwin, the youngest of five brothers, all of whom are actors, owed $400,000 in back taxes and was taken to court for it in 2013. The *Usual Suspects* star managed to avoid jail time by admitting that he failed to pay New York State taxes, and under a plea deal he was given one year to pay back the money.

Wesley Snipes wasn't so lucky. In 2006, he was charged with one count of conspiring to defraud the United States government, the IRS claiming that he used accountants with a history of filing false returns. While he was acquitted of fraud, he was still found guilty of failing to file federal income tax returns, and ultimately served a three-year prison sentence.

Paying taxes is the law of the land in the United States, and if millions of people who make less than the NBA minimum salary of $507,366 pay their taxes every year and go on with their lives, actors and athletes have no excuse not to do the same.

--------- TIPS ---------

1. Find a professional to help prepare and file your taxes.
2. Pay taxes on time and in full. Paying late will only cost you in penalties and fees.

3. Remember that side income is taxable.

4. Maintain accurate financial records. Everyone loves cash, but cash can be hard to keep track of if you don't keep all your receipts.

5. Take as many tax deductions as possible. The more tax deductions you claim, the less you pay.

6. Invest the maximum in your 401(k) and other pension plans.

7. If you generate enough money on the side, establish a Limited Liability Company (LLC).

Most people hate paying taxes, mainly because they feel they're paying out too large a percentage of what they earn. I, personally, don't mind paying taxes, because I like driving my car on well-maintained roads. I like that the fire department will come to my house if there's an emergency. I like it when the cops stop by to see if I'm okay after my home alarm goes off. I like kids having access to a good public education.

You shouldn't try to avoid paying taxes. From your first day as an income-earning individual, you need to pay. Not paying taxes can have a negative effect on your financial outlook and opens you up to criminal penalties and even jail time. Plain and simple: Don't mess with Uncle Sam.

THE PLAYERS

BIG BALLER TOM

Big Baller Tom lives in California and pays a high state income tax. In California the state tax is 13.3 percent.

Remaining Income:	$5,052,760
Federal Tax (35%):	−$2,582,216
State Tax (13.3%):	−$981,242
Income after Taxes:	$1,489,302

STEADY· JOHN

Steady John decided to live in Florida, which means he pays no state income tax.

Remaining Income:	$6,223,760
Federal Tax (35%):	−$2,237,466
State Tax (0%):	$0
Income after Taxes:	$3,986,294

CHAPTER SEVEN

CONTROLLING THE REBOUND

ALIMONY AND CHILD SUPPORT

In the mid-1990s, R&B singer Brandy Norwood was emerging as a star. *Brandy*, her 1994 debut album, was dominating the radio—it had produced four *Billboard* Top Ten hits, including two number ones. By January 1996, she was starring in a prime-time sitcom, *Moesha*. With all of that going on for her at just seventeen, you can imagine how hard it would be for a seventeen-year-old boy to approach her, let alone ask her to go to his prom, but that's just what happened when high school senior Kobe Bryant ran into her in New York City.

She said yes.

Kobe was in New York to receive an *Essence* magazine award as the top high school player in the country, so even then he wasn't exactly a nobody. But Brandy, though she was an international star, actually *jumped* at the chance to go with him. Prom night turned out to be something of a spectacle, with more media coverage than high school proms usually garner, but Kobe and Brandy were able to spend some time alone and block everything out and have a good time like regular kids.

From the time they're in junior high school, boys who appear to have the talent to make it to the NBA are treated like celebrities. As they move into high school, attracting women comes easily to them. Girls in high school, like women in college, are drawn to celebrity, making it easy for these athletes to meet and date practically any woman they want. Because of this, professional athletes have access to some of the most beautiful women around. Of course, beautiful doesn't always equate with compatible, but that doesn't stop players from marrying women who may have been more interested in their celebrity than in who they actually are.

Marriage in this country is a fifty-fifty proposition at best. The divorce rate is high across every demographic, including professional athletes. Aside from being emotionally challenging, a divorce can also be expensive. Michael Jordan, who married his wife with no prenuptial agreement, ended up having to pay her $168 million. When golfer Tiger Woods's cheating was exposed, it cost him his marriage and $165 million.

Deion Sanders had a prenup stipulating that upon divorce, he would buy his spouse a home valued at half the worth of the house they were living in at the time of the divorce. When the marriage dissolved, they were living in a $20 million home, and Sanders had to buy a $10 million house for his ex.

Then there's former New York Giant Michael Strahan, who had to give his wife $15.5 million when they divorced.

At the time, that was about half of his net worth. He was also ordered to pay $180,000 a month for child support, although a couple of years later a court determined that the support had been miscalculated and that he should have been paying only $2,424 a month.

Early in my career, I heard a league official say that once they retire, there is an 87 percent divorce rate among NBA players. Although I haven't verified this number, based on what I've witnessed, it seems about right.

What *is* fact is that 40 to 50 percent of all marriages in America end in divorce within ten years. So, if you are planning to get married, make sure that you also plan for divorce. Even with a solid prenup, a divorce is not free. It is going to cost you.

I recommend marrying a seasoned professional, someone who has already figured out her direction in life and is on a path to achieving her goals. I reason that it makes it much more likely she'll be too busy with her own life to worry about new ways to spend my money.

Pro athletes have to be careful. It's widely known that a good number of athletes cheat on their spouses or long-term girlfriends. It's a reality that some argue is human nature. I don't think it is human nature. I'm convinced that it is common for men to cheat partly because the infidelity is tolerated by their spouse. I believe most athletes' wives accept that their husbands are cheating, but often let it go because they don't want to give up the lifestyle to which they've become accustomed—the mansions, fancy cars, clothes, shopping sprees, and luxurious vacations.

There's also the recognition that is appealing. Team players' wives are offered preferred seating in sports arenas and restaurants and are given celebrity treatment when shopping at high-end stores. These women are viewed as celebrities by virtue of being married to one. Who wants to give that up?

On reality shows like *Basketball Wives* and *Basketball Wives LA*, the majority of the women are no longer married to NBA players, yet they retain celebrity status. Some NBA wives simply put in their time and wait for their investment to mature, all the while gathering evidence on infidelity. Once their husband has reached his maximum earning potential, they'll file for divorce.

AFTER THE LOVE IS GONE

People file for divorce for all kinds of reasons, including extramarital affairs, money, lack of communication, and even weight gain. Any of these issues can come to the forefront once a player is at home every day, and if you combine that with the fact that less money is coming in, the situation can get tense. While a player's career is active, his wife may have overlooked his cheating or the fact that he just didn't listen to anything she had to say, but with him at home every day, she may not be as willing to let things go. Meanwhile, as a retired player, he's not going to be working out regularly and could start putting on some pounds, looking less and less each day like the man she married. Combine all of this, and a lot of wives get fed up and file for divorce.

After retirement, people's lives change. When a pro athlete's schedule finally allows him to spend quality time with his wife at home, he's forced to handle day-to-day issues that in the past he was able to run away from. Whether it's how to deal with the guests coming over for Thanksgiving or why there are messages on the answering machine from some woman, his schedule with the team made it very easy for him to evade discussions around these matters. Because of the amount of time spent on the road during their playing days, most retired athletes didn't have a clear role in the household—the wife was the chief of the house. Now that he is there, he may want a larger role, but exactly what that is can be hard to define after all the years that he wasn't really around.

As we know, many people will experience a divorce in their lifetime, and an alarming number of couples don't have a prenup. People are afraid of approaching the subject of a prenup, for a number of reasons. First, they don't want their significant others to think they don't love them. Second, they worry that it puts a curse on the relationship from the beginning. Third, and perhaps worst, they're afraid their significant other won't sign the agreement and will end the relationship. These are all legitimate concerns, but consider the alternative. If you get married without one, you could end up in a situation where you've spent your entire career working hard, only to retire and face divorce and the loss of your wealth.

In a notorious story, Stephen Jackson, perhaps best known for his role in the Indiana Pacers' fight with the fans, waited until the day of the wedding to get his prenuptial agreement signed. His fiancée, Imani Showalter, refused, so the wedding was called off, even though guests had already begun arriving. Obviously, there is a better time to present your partner with a prenuptial agreement—but it is one hundred percent reasonable to want to protect your assets should something happen to your marriage.

Here is a short list of reasons you should consider signing a prenup. If you fall into any of the following categories, you need to have one, and there's not really any room for arguing about it.

+ You have assets such as a home, stock, or retirement funds.
+ You own all or part of a business.
+ You receive an inheritance or will in the future.
+ You have children and/or grandchildren from a previous marriage.
+ One spouse is much wealthier than the other.
+ One spouse will be supporting the other through college.
+ You have loved ones, such as elderly parents, who need to be taken care of financially.
+ You have or are pursuing a degree or license in a potentially lucrative profession.

Now, let's look at what a prenup actually does:

+ Maintains separate finances
+ Protects against a spouse's debt
+ Provides for children from prior relationships

+ Maintains property in the family
+ Defines who gets what in case of a divorce

Without a prenup, state law will specify how your property will be divided in the event of a divorce. These laws may dictate a result that neither of you wants. You can use a prenup to establish your own rules for property division and avoid potential disagreements. In most states, you can also make agreements about whether or not one or both of you will be entitled to alimony.

In addition to the things listed above, there are other matters people include in their prenups, such as whether to file joint or separate income tax returns, how to allocate income, child-care and educational responsibilities, how you will relate to in-laws or stepchildren, or, if there are pets, who will be responsible for them.

If you plan on getting married, at the very least you should see a lawyer to discuss your plans and what your prenup should look like. Remember, each state has different prenup rules.

Divorce has become all too common in our society, so it only makes sense to protect yourself from the pitfalls of one long before it ever happens.

Top athletes often jeopardize their marriages and their finances by having relationships with multiple women simultaneously. A great number of pro ballers view women as throwaway objects or as things to conquer. And then there are the groupies. Groupies are women whose sole intent is to meet and marry a high-income professional athlete. These women know how to make themselves available. By that, I mean that if you are living a pro athlete's life, groupies are at games, team events, parties, and clubs.

NBA All-Star Weekend is a good example. As you get to the hotel in whatever city the NBA is holding its annual celebration, you see the lobby littered with groupies, though, based on the way they dress, it may be a little difficult for the uninitiated to differentiate between the groupies and the hookers. The groupies are there to meet players, or anyone else who appears to have money and access to the players. There are groupies who simply want to hook up with a player for a one-night stand, and there are others who are looking to take it to the next level and get married or at least engaged to a rich baller. There are also groupies who are perfectly happy just getting pregnant by one.

No one is in the bedroom with them, so why more athletes don't protect themselves against accidental pregnancies is a question that is difficult to answer with certainty. The reasons could be as numerous as there are athletes with out-of-wedlock children, but no matter the explanation, a very high percentage of athletes have children out of wedlock. Bringing a child into the world with a woman whom you viewed only as an object to be conquered is no way to do it. These relationships are usually not built on any kind of foundation, and more often than not they end relatively quickly, if a relationship ever materializes at all. Needless to say, this is a situation that will probably end up in family court, with a judge deciding how much money the athlete will have to pay to the woman to raise his child. So, who conquered whom?

Raising children is expensive, and it is particularly costly for professional athletes who have children out of wedlock. A 1998 *Sports Illustrated* issue ran a story about the insane number of illegitimate children professional athletes have. An NBA player's agent told the magazine that he spends more time dealing with paternity claims than he does negotiating contracts. The agent also believed that NBA players may be responsible for more kids born out of wedlock than there are players in the NBA.

Having children out of wedlock is a personal issue, and I'm not making any moral judgments about it. But I *am* making a case regarding the best interests of the child, as well as the father's financial health, and neither is a good situation. The majority of men I see around sports who deal with economic distress and even financial ruin typically owe their misfortune to bringing children into the world with multiple women.

Big-money athletes are often warned to steer clear of groupies and other women who may want to marry them or just have a baby in order to secure their own financial freedom in the form of child support payments. Unfortunately, too many athletes are not heeding this advice. The evidence of this is right there in the family room at any NBA arena, where after a game it looks like a day care center. Of course, this could be avoided if athletes would simply use protection when having sex. A condom can go a long way in preventing unwanted pregnancies and protecting against sexually transmitted diseases. Again, since no one is in the bedroom with the couple, why so many pro ball players do not use condoms is a question that I'm not going to be able to answer here.

While this phenomenon of using child support as adult support is often discussed, analyzed, and even judged, it's not just the superwealthy who can be targeted. Whether you're a man or a woman, don't underestimate your worth. Your having a solid income and a bright future is enough for someone else to try to take advantage of you. There are people who will do anything to attach themselves to your success, no matter how moderate you may deem it to be. While it's true that a doctor running his own practice could be a target, a bus driver could be as well. Because a bus driver is generally in a union, he will earn a pretty good salary and have great benefits and a pension. More important, it's hard for him to get fired, based on the protection his union provides. There are women who know this and who will not hesitate to go down to family court and file to get a chunk of his weekly salary in the form of child support.

Women may be the ones chasing athletes around, but there are both men and women who will try to link themselves to a bright young banker, lawyer, or registered nurse. All I can say here is that before becoming romantically involved with someone, do all you can to get to know that person well. If he or she has ulterior motives, hopefully you'll be able to figure that out during the time you're able to spend together prior to getting into the bedroom.

Child support is expensive. States use varying methods to determine the amount of support the noncustodial parent—or the parent with whom the child does not live—

would have to pay. Whatever method they use, you will *feel* the amount. In other words, in an intact family, you can budget exactly how much money you spend on your child, but once you're in court, a judge determines how much you'll pay, and believe me, it is going to be more—much more—than you would have budgeted, and certainly more than the actual cost of raising a child.

Court-ordered child support is more expensive than the actual cost of raising a child for a few reasons. First, the noncustodial parent is paying for the child's portion of the utilities at the custodial parent's home, because in theory if the child were not living there, the house would need less heat, electricity, and water. Next, the custodial parent will have to have an additional bedroom for the child, so a percentage of the additional rent or mortgage payment for the larger house is worked in. Finally, the support order is covering a portion of the child's food as well.

Meanwhile, the noncustodial parent has to have an additional room as well for when the child visits, but the money he may have had for that is paying for his ex's house to be larger. So he ends up paying twice for the child to have a bedroom. And with the extra bedroom come the extra utility expense, as it takes more heat to warm two bedrooms than one. Then there's the food. It is much more expensive to buy food for yourself and then separately buy food for your child than it is to share food like people do when they're living in the same house. Yet once you're paying child support, that's exactly what you're doing.

Most states use one of two formulas to determine the

amount of money that a noncustodial parent, also known as the obligor, has to pay. The Income Shares Model is preferred by most states, while some states use the Percentage of Income Model. Either way, the goal is to ensure that children of divorced or never-married parents will enjoy the lifestyle they would have had were the family still intact. Both models increase the percentages slightly as the number of children involved rises. In other words, a noncustodial parent will have to pay more for two children than she would for one. The amount would rise as the number of children rose. For ease of calculating, we'll assume there is just one child.

The Income Shares Model combines the gross income of both parents, and based on that amount assigns a percentage of that total to go to the child. The percentage of your combined gross incomes that should go to your child goes down as the income goes up. So, if the combined gross is between $21,000 and $28,000, the court would determine that 23.7 percent of that should go to the child. Under $40,000 would yield 22.9 percent, and if the income is over $51,000, then 17.8 percent would be assigned.

Based on an annual income of $36,750 for you as a noncustodial parent and $30,000 as the other parent's yearly earnings, the two of you would have a combined gross income of $66,750. The formula's guidelines assign 17.8 percent of that, or $11,881.50, to be spent on the child. Since your $36,750 represents 55 percent of the combined gross income, you are responsible for 55 percent of the amount that is to go to your child. In this case, that would be $6,534.82 per year, or $136.14 every week.

Now, if you think back to the chapter on income, after your basic necessities, that $36,750 salary left you with $119.76 per week, from which you still had to buy clothes and save for retirement. So, with a court order for $136.14 weekly in child support and only $119.76 in your pocket, you're already $65.52 in the negative each month.

There are other factors as well. If you have a small child, most states will add the cost of day care to the final support amount and use the same percentage method to figure out how much of that you will pay. The cost for full-time day care at an accredited facility varies widely, depending on where you live and the age of the child. If you live in Mississippi, the average day care will cost you around $5,000 a year, but in New York State, the average cost is closer to $15,000. If there is a day care center that your child is already attending, the court will use the exact numbers that the facility charges. The average amount for the United States is $11,666 per year. Using that number, you would be responsible for 55 percent, or $6,413.30 a year, to pay for your child's day care. That breaks down to $534.44 a month, or $133.61 each week. This is on top of the $136.14 that you already have to pay for child support.

With a child young enough for day care, you are looking at a total child support order for $269.75 each week. That $119.75 you had to spend is looking very inadequate right about now. How on earth are you supposed to pay $269.75 every week when you have less than $120? Not only would this take up the little disposable income you had, it would eat right into the money you need to pay for your basic necessities.

The courts are not forgiving just because you will be unable to make a decent living. Their only concern is the amount of money that you will have to pay under the order; there is no concern about whether or not you will be able to take care of yourself after paying it.

States aggressively enforce support orders, too. If you are working, the support amount is usually an automatic wage garnishment from the day of the order. It doesn't work as it does with other creditors, to whom you'd have to owe a lot of money before they could finally take you to court, win a judgment, and have your wages garnished. The automatic wage garnishment also exposes your personal business to your employer, who will receive an order to deduct a specific amount from your check each pay period and send it to the court.

If you don't have a payroll job, you are responsible for sending the money, and if you fall behind, you are charged interest on the unpaid balance. If you fall way behind, the court may suspend your driver's license or any other professional license you may have, like a fishing and gaming license, or even your license to practice medicine. Beyond that, obligors who owe large amounts of support are routinely put in jail until they pay a certain amount. The only problem is, sitting in jail, how are you supposed to make any money to pay the arrears? This is how grown men with jobs end up living in their parents' home. Is that what you really want?

With your paying 55 percent of the child care costs, the custodial parent is responsible for 45 percent. However, there is no court order written for the custodial parent, because it is assumed that parent will pay what is required since the child is living with her. The custodial parent never has to provide proof of any money spent, and if she doesn't spend what she is supposed to, there are no penalties.

The Percentage of Income Model is much simpler to calculate, but yields similar results. This model looks at the gross income of the noncustodial parent and takes a percentage of it for the support; the noncustodial parent's income never comes into the equation. Seventeen percent is taken for one child, and 23 percent for two. Twenty-nine percent is taken for three children, 31 percent for four, and 34 percent for five or more kids. If you have children with more than one woman, then it's a race to family court. The first woman to file would get 17 percent of your gross salary. The next to file would get 17 percent of your remaining salary after the first court order. With a yearly salary of $36,750 in a state using the Percentage of Income Model, for one child, you would have to pay $130.15 each week. The major difference between the models is that this one does not add the cost of day care to the order.

For high earners, all of this goes out the window. If a noncustodial parent makes more than $80,000 or so a year, the judge will not use the guidelines and will instead just try to figure out what the expenses are. If you live in a million-dollar home, then the judge will try to figure out what has to be done so that your child and the other parent can live in a million-dollar home as well. If you can afford that home, the court will assume you can pay for private school. You have a Mercedes-Benz? How can we get your ex into a Benz so that when your child rides around, it will be in a Benz? At this point, you would end up paying nearly double for everything. This is how all these famous athletes and entertainers end up paying ungodly amounts in child support.

If you are taken to court for child support while under an NBA contract, the order can be anywhere from $5,000 to $30,000 per month. This obligation can continue for eighteen years in some states and twenty-one in others. If you don't navigate the court system properly, it'll go on even when your career is over and the big bucks have stopped rolling in. Imagine paying $10,000 a month in child support. That's $120,000 a year! After eighteen years, a father who hasn't even seen his child enough to build a solid bond may have paid $2.1 million or more for her upbringing.

Court-ordered child support takes a large chunk of money from high earners, but they're still able to live their life. An average earner might not be so lucky. That chunk of child support will absolutely change your lifestyle, and may even leave you unable to afford to marry and raise a family.

If you don't have the salary of a pro athlete, child support can cripple you. As mentioned, oftentimes support is ordered in an amount that the noncustodial parent simply cannot afford. Some like to say that noncustodial parents can't afford to pay *and* maintain their lifestyle, but the reality is, support is often set so high that after paying it, these parents don't have enough money to pay rent or bills *anywhere*, let alone maintain whatever lifestyle they previously enjoyed.

You can either pay child support or pay your rent. Of

course, if you choose to pay your rent, there will be an arrest warrant out for you for not paying the support. If you pay the support and end up homeless, no one will care other than possibly your parents.

Even worse, sometimes women who have children with men they're not married to make it difficult for them to be a good father. Since the woman's financial security is at stake, she may keep the father at arm's length, controlling his visits based on his fulfillment of financial obligations set by the court. While the court makes it clear that this is unacceptable, there is no recourse for the father if the behavior presents itself. There is no real way for the court to enforce visitation violations absent of putting the mother in jail, and no judge wants to do that because most judges feel as though they would be taking a parent away from her children.

It was a pretty big news story back in 2012 when Miami Heat star Dwyane Wade's ex-wife, Siohvaughn, was charged with child abduction, visitation interference, and resisting arrest. During Father's Day weekend of that year, Dwyane's sister arrived at Siohvaughn's house to pick up the couple's two sons and bring them home to Dwyane, who had been awarded custody. But Siohvaughn was nowhere to be found. Neither were the boys. A few hours later, Dwyane's sister showed up again with the sheriff, and this time Siohvaughn was there but refused to open the door. When she finally tried to leave the premises (without the children, who were inside), she was arrested.

Dwyane and Siohvaughn, high school sweethearts, separated in 2007 and were divorced in 2010, and in March 2011

Dwyane was awarded sole custody of the boys after Sioh-vaughn was found to have repeatedly used the children as pawns in her battle against him. In July 2010, a warrant had been issued for Siohvaughn's arrest after she failed to show up in court for a hearing. The judge in the case was upset by the fact that her lawyers were unable to reach her. They also noted that prior to that scheduled appearance, she had not made the boys available for daily phone conversations with their father, as had been ordered by the court, and that the kids weren't at their school to be picked up by Dwyane's sister, as had also been ordered. Dwyane's lawyer added that Siohvaughn once called the police when Dwyane showed up at their Miami home to pick up the children, falsely telling the cops that there was a warrant out for his arrest.

Most men are not able to successfully navigate something like this in court. If you don't have the money a Dwyane Wade has, the court will pay only cursory attention to your claims. It is not going to issue an arrest warrant for a mother, and it certainly isn't going to change the terms of a custody agreement because she is denying you access to your children. It is much more likely that the court will not be able to do anything about visitation denials. However, if you fall behind on your child support payments, it will certainly enforce that.

There is no shortage of crazy, dramatic child support stories. You may remember that back in 2005 P. Diddy was ordered to pay the largest child support award in New York

State history. The court was responding to a suit filed by his ex-girlfriend, Misa Hylton-Brim, asking for $35,000 a month. He was ordered to pay $21,782, a quadruple increase from the $5,112 he had been paying for their son. In addition to the humongous amount, the music mogul also had to pay for his son's health insurance, tuition, vacations, and clothes, which kind of makes you wonder what the $21,000 is covering.

Meanwhile, Diddy was already paying $20,000 a month to his other ex, model Kim Porter, with whom he also had one son. Porter had taken him to court in 2001 and gotten the $20,000 order. Now, in 2005, between the two orders, Diddy was paying close to $42,000 for child support every month. There were rumors that Hylton-Brim had been upset that she was getting only $5,000 while Porter was getting $20,000 and that she sued Diddy for that reason. This may or may not be true, as she claimed at the time that she needed the money to care for the boy, but either way, having children out of wedlock subjects you to that sort of claim, whether it's legitimate or just whimsical.

Jason Caffey earned nearly $35 million over eight NBA seasons and has a total of ten children from eight women. In 2007, he was arrested for not paying child support. He was $200,000 in arrears and had to file for bankruptcy to protect himself from his creditors. But bankruptcy does not protect you from child support obligations.

It is confirmed that Shawn Kemp has seven kids by six different women. It is rumored, however, that there might be more. As a result of this and some other issues, he has experienced a great deal of financial distress, despite having earned a reported $91 million in salary during his NBA career and millions more from product endorsements.

In December 2001, Antoine Walker was accused of not paying child support for his youngest daughter. It was also revealed that he owed $27,817 to the University of Chicago Laboratory Schools for her tuition. According to the girl's mother, he hadn't made his $4,195 monthly child support payments in more than two years. All this came a year *after* he had filed for bankruptcy.

Dennis Rodman's lawyers recently told a judge he was "broke" and "suffering from a drinking problem" to try to spare him from paying more than $800,000 he owed in back child support. The two sides settled on $500,000 as the amount he'll have to pay back. In the meantime, the regular payments continue—the half a million dollars has to be paid back to his ex-wife, Michelle Rodman, while he is still making his normal $50,000 monthly payments.

Former heavyweight champion boxer Evander Holyfield lost more than $250 million on everything from failed record labels to video game companies. He has eleven kids and owes quite a bit in child support. At one point a Georgia judge ordered him to pay $2,950 a month to pay off $563,900.91 in back child support for just *one* of those children.

Athletes don't have to be big stars to get in trouble for child support. Tyrone Nesby played in the NBA from 1999 to 2002. In 2011, he was ordered to pay nearly $1 million in back child support and sentenced to five years of probation. He was also strongly encouraged to speak to children about the importance of family and the lessons he learned as a result of his not paying child support.

These examples are just a small sampling of the consequences of having children out of wedlock. Make no mistake, though: No matter how well-off you may be, having to come up with this level of financial support for even just one child is huge and could drain anyone's financial resources.

TIPS

1. Be faithful. If you can't stop sleeping around, then don't get married.
2. If you are planning to get married, obtain a prenuptial agreement.
3. Wear a damn condom. Protect yourself from conceiving unplanned children.
4. When dealing with child support issues, get a good lawyer. Do not enter family court without one.
5. If your income changes, you can file a petition with the court to lower the amount of child support you pay.
6. If the mother of your child doesn't initially take you to court, be generous with the amount of money that you give her for the child. No matter what amount you give, it will be better than dealing with the court.
7. Get to know someone before opening yourself up to be taken advantage of. Hopefully, you'll be able to determine what her true motives are before it's too late.

I believe NBA players can have good relationships with decent women who don't simply want to use them for financial support, but based on my experience, these relationships are few and far between. It is much easier for a pro athlete, especially an NBA player, to get hooked up with a groupie than with a woman who has her own career and is able to care for herself emotionally and financially.

Women who would make for better wives are generally not at the parties or restaurants or even All-Star Weekend events where players can be found. So, players need to wise up, make good decisions, take control of their lives, and do everything they can to avoid joining the high number of athletes with multiple unplanned and out-of-wedlock children.

The same is true for non-athletes. It's just as important for you to make good decisions as it is for a big-money pro baller.

THE PLAYERS

Divorce has become all too common in our society, so it only makes sense to protect yourself from the pitfalls of a divorce long before it ever happens.

BIG BALLER TOM

Big Baller Tom is married but did not present his wife with a prenup because he was afraid she wouldn't sign it. This leaves him vulnerable to losing half of his income in the event of a divorce. Tom also has three children with three other women, and is paying child support to all of them.

Remaining Income:	$1,489,302
Divorce Expense:	$0

CHILD SUPPORT

Luck: −$10,000 × 36 months = −$360,000

Duce: −$10,000 × 36 months = −$360,000

Sally: −$10,000 × 36 months = −$360,000

Total Child Support:	−$1,080,000

Income After Child Support:	$409,302

STEADY JOHN

Steady John is married with one child. His wife signed a prenup before they got married, which will protect the majority of his wealth in the event of a divorce. Since he lives with his wife and baby, he pays no child support. Needless to say, he still incurs expenses related to school, food, clothes, a nanny, etc.

Remaining Income:	$3,986,294
Divorce Expense:	$0
Child Support (−$20,000 × 3 years):	−$60,000

Income after Child Support:	$3,926,294

CHAPTER EIGHT

THE INJURED LIST

ADDRESSING MEDICAL EXPENSES

A lonzo Mourning was a star center at Georgetown before playing in the NBA for the Charlotte Hornets and later the Miami Heat and New Jersey Nets. Over the course of his fifteen NBA seasons, he averaged seventeen points, eight rebounds, and nearly three blocks per game. In Charlotte he combined with power forward Larry Johnson to make up one the most formidable frontcourts of the '90s. One of the best players in the NBA and still relatively young, in 2003 he was diagnosed with glomerulosclerosis, a degenerative disease usually associated with diabetes or hardening of the arteries within the kidneys. Later that year, he had a kidney transplant, which should have effectively ended his career.

But Alonzo came back. He returned to the court and the Miami Heat, where he picked up right where he left off, anchoring the defense for Pat Riley's team. In 2007, playing in his fifteenth season, 'Zo was going up to defend the basket as Atlanta's Mario West came off a screen and was driving down the lane, when, as far as Alonzo could tell, his foot slipped as he planted himself to jump. Replays show that he didn't slip, nor was there contact with West. Mourning's knee merely buckled, and he tore the patellar tendon in his right knee.

Alonzo knew that his career was over. Medical personnel came onto the court and placed him on a stretcher, but he refused the ride as he kept repeating, "It's over, it's over."

'Zo got up, took a slow, painful, and deliberate walk back to the bench, and never played again. About the stretcher, he later said, "That's not the way I envisioned myself walking off the court for the last time in my career. . . . If I had to crawl off the court I would have. Nobody was going to push me on a stretcher off the court. That wasn't going to happen."

Injuries are the main reason athletes retire. If you leave it up to the player, he will stay in the game until he has to be carried off. You don't have to meet many retired athletes to learn that very few of them actually walked away on their own terms and injury-free. Most retired pros have some sort of limp or pain in their back when they do certain activities. Many have had several surgeries throughout the course of their career, and it's always astounded me that a pro athlete may have had ten or eleven surgeries by the time he's thirty.

Perhaps you saw New York Yankee Derek Jeter take his "victory lap" around the league during the 2014 summer. Jeter is one of the very few athletes who was able to retire when he wanted to, and on his own terms. He closed out his career with no major injuries and announced his retirement a year ahead of time, intentionally or unintentionally allowing every other team in the league to capitalize on his last visit to their park. Everyone wants to retire like Jeter, but most of the time that just isn't possible.

Injuries ultimately break every athlete's body down—it's just the nature of getting older. I had issues with my knees dating all the way back to my college days, resulting in several surgeries over the years in order for me to be able to stay on the court. One summer while I was still playing in the league, I was in a pickup game with some other guys at UC Berkeley. I grabbed a rebound, passed it out quickly, and then sprinted upcourt to get into the play on the offensive end just like I had done thousands, if not hundreds of thousands, of times before. But this time was different. Running down the floor, I heard my knee pop. It sounded like it was coming from somewhere else, but since the pain shot up my leg, I knew exactly where it had originated. I had an operation to repair the joint and continued my NBA career for several years.

Then one day I was again at a gym in Los Angeles working out with my old teammate Dwight Howard. At a certain point, we were playing one-on-one. I pulled up for a fadeaway, heard a pop and then felt everything in my knee go out. It was just like the last time. I knew right away, just as Alonzo had several years earlier. I turned around and told my assistant that my career was over. It's something about those knees. When your knee goes, you know it.

My story is not atypical. Many players leave the sport at an early age due to injury. As a result of those injuries, athletes may continue to have enormous medical expenses throughout the rest of their life. It's not just players in their thirties, either. Greg Oden, in 2007 the No. 1 overall pick out of Ohio State, had to retire by his fourth year in the league (although he did make a return in 2014). His teammate, Brandon Roy, was a three-time All-Star by age twenty-five before having his career shattered by injury at twenty-six. Chris Taft played one year in the NBA and showed promise before badly injuring his back during a summer league game. He continues to try to stage a comeback. And then there's Yao Ming. An eight-time All-Star and one of the best big men in the game, he appeared in only five games after the age of twenty-eight, due to chronic foot injuries, and is now retired.

Medical benefits take care of you while you are playing, because just as in any other job, your team is your employer and provides health care. But once you retire you're on your own, so it is important to plan for medical expenses that may come up during retirement. The career of a pro athlete is so short that he will typically have thirty years or more from the time he retires until he is eligible for Medicare, the government-backed health insurance plan that all Americans over the age of sixty-five are eligible for.

Medicare currently covers only around 62 percent of an individual's medical expenses. What's worse is that the percentage of expenses it covers is predicted to go down. Because individuals' health care costs are rising, it's more important than ever to plan for these expenses in retirement. The average out-of-pocket cost of health care in 2011 for a sixty-five-year-old on Medicare was close to $4,600, while for a seventy-five-year-old those costs jumped to $5,400, so even with Medicare, health insurance can be costly. This is why it is so important to account for these costs as you are making your retirement plan. A financial adviser can tell you exactly how to do this. Some employers provide some level of health insurance after you retire, but you'd have to check with your company's human resources department to find out if yours is one of them.

You may also plan to work part-time during the early years of your retirement. That way, you can limit the amount of money you withdraw from your retirement account and pay out of pocket for any expenses that may arise. Since you would be drawing an income, you should plan to save some of that money just as you did in your younger years.

For pro athletes, much more money would have to be allotted for medical costs because, as I mentioned before, there is often a thirty-year gap between retirement and Medicare eligibility. Most players get other jobs during those years, with the TV analysts being the most high profile. A job working for a TV network will surely offer medical benefits, thus reducing the amount of money you'd have to spend on care. Some athletes get much lower-profile jobs, and, in this day and age, whether or not these jobs will offer health care is a toss-up.

Adrian Dantley is widely regarded as among the best pure scorers the league has ever seen. His six-foot-five frame made him a true "tweener"—too big to play guard and too small to play forward—yet he found a way to get the ball in the basket. Dantley played with the Utah Jazz and the Detroit Pistons in the '80s before retiring in 1991 after fifteen seasons, his 23,177 points making him the ninth-leading scorer in NBA history up to that time.

These days, Dantley lives in a home he purchased for $1.1 million in 1991, not far from where he went to high school in Silver Spring, Maryland. He also works a part-time job as a school crossing guard at nearby Eastern Middle School. The job pays just $14,685.50 a year, money he doesn't need, as he always took care of his earnings when he was playing. What he enjoys about the job, besides the kids, are the health benefits. You see, in Montgomery County, a crossing guard is a part-time job that offers full-time benefits. While Dantley may have his finances in order, why should he pay for health benefits when he can merely go a couple of miles to work one hour in the morning and one hour in the afternoon and have it paid for? He even has summers off, just like when he was playing basketball.

Health care in this country is expensive and difficult for anyone to navigate. For pro athletes, many of whom have issues with concussions, bone spurs, unstable backs, broken joints, etc., the cost of maintaining a healthy body is significant. Medical expenses can gradually deplete their assets. Repair those knees? Have that back surgery? Scope that arthritic ankle? These postcareer medical expenditures can take a chunk out of what they earned. Because of this, the NBA and the NBPA have launched a medical reimbursement plan, in which the NBA and the union each contribute to a fund that covers medical expenses for players after they retire.

Athletes in every sport get injured, but football is the scariest. During the 2010 college football season, Rutgers junior defensive tackle Eric LeGrand suffered a spinal-cord injury during a 23–20 overtime win over Army. With just over five minutes remaining in the game, LeGrand was attempting to make a tackle on a kickoff and collided with Army's Malcolm Brown. After the play, Eric didn't get up. As medical professionals and teammates gathered around, he lay there without moving for several minutes before he was finally carted off the field. It was later revealed that LeGrand had been paralyzed from the neck down.

What had seemed like a routine play ended LeGrand's life as he knew it. Eventually he regained motion in his arms, but he remains paralyzed below the waist. Greg Schiano, his coach at Rutgers, moved on and got hired as the head coach of the NFL's Tampa Bay Buccaneers. When the team was pulling together their ninety-man off-season roster for 2012, Schiano reached out to LeGrand and signed him to the squad, helping Eric fulfill his dream of signing with an NFL team.

David Wilson, who played for the New York Giants in 2012 and 2013, injured his neck in a game against the Philadelphia Eagles in 2013, missing the rest of the season. He had spinal fusion surgery in January 2014 and eventually was diagnosed with diffuse cervical stenosis. Doctors told him then that he should never play again.

Michael Irvin, the NFL Network analyst who won three Super Bowls with the Cowboys in the '90s, had his career end on a hit he took at Veterans Stadium in Philadelphia. He lay motionless on the turf for some very scary moments before being taken off the field on a stretcher.

Injuries in football are so common and severe that a group

of former NFL players have sued their players' union for not providing accurate information about the risk of head injuries. The players claim the NFL Players Association "withheld information from the players about the risks of head injuries." As relief, the players have asked the court for medical monitoring and compensation for the costs of treating long-term chronic injuries and other financial losses.

Just because you've never played in the NFL doesn't mean you're off the hook. You don't have to be a pro athlete to develop chronic back pain in your late thirties or early forties. When aches, pains, and other medical issues creep in, your health care expenses start to rise. Old injuries catch up to you and new ones develop—older men tend to develop such health concerns as diabetes, heart disease, or high blood pressure. Each health issue you have requires its own set of doctor's visits, treatments, and prescriptions. But as long as you're working, your insurance should cover most anything that may come up.

Medical insurance pays for any health care expenses that you may have, such as visiting your primary doctor or any kind of specialist. Suppose you sprain your wrist and need to see a chiropractor—your insurance will cover that. But be aware that not every doctor accepts every kind of insurance, so before choosing the insurance you are going to use, check with your doctor's office to be sure it's accepted there. If it isn't, it's worth it for you to choose another company or plan. In the end, the various companies are not that different from the consumer's point of view, but if you've been seeing a doctor for a number of years, then he's one of a kind.

Dental and vision plans usually have their own separate packages but will still fall under your employer's overall health coverage. Again, you should check with your dentist and eye doctor to find out if they accept the insurance you're about to select. Health insurance will also pay if you have to go to the emergency room. It can reimburse you for care you have paid for out of your pocket, but in most cases it pays the doctor or hospital directly.

For people who don't work at a company that provides health benefits, in 2013 the U.S. government put a new health system, the Affordable Care Act (ACA), into operation. You might have heard people referring to this as Obamacare. That is not the official name of the new health care system, but this is what they're referring to. Under the ACA, if you're an American citizen, you can now purchase a health care plan on your own and, based on your income, the cost will be brought into line with what you would be paying if you were receiving employer-based coverage. Prior to this, health insurance was unaffordable for most people who didn't have employer-based health coverage. The information used to determine the amount you'll have to pay is taken from your tax filing, so make sure to get your taxes in on time and professionally prepared.

TIPS

1. If you have a medical reimbursement account, you should make sure to not spend that money while you're in the league. Leave it for retirement.

2. Plan for medical expenses that may come up after retirement.

3. Be aware that medical costs go up as you get older.

4. Remember, after age sixty-five, you can still have out-of-pocket medical expenses.

5. Consider working part-time if benefits are available, or to save and invest the money you earn.

6. Make sure your doctor accepts the insurance you plan to select.

7. If you are self-employed or if your employer does not offer health insurance, take advantage of the Affordable Care Act.

Professional sports leagues owe a debt of gratitude to the men and women who play their hearts out and leave the game with their bodies broken down. It's irresponsible to not help these players beyond their years of service. I applaud the NBA and NBPA for establishing a medical reimbursement account. I hope that every other league follows suit. However, all athletes have to know that it is ultimately their responsibility to care for themselves upon retirement. Therefore, it is imperative to save money for medical care, not only for your survival, but also for your quality of life after you hang up your uniform.

THE PLAYERS

Both athletes have a medical reimbursement account into which the league and the union contribute each year. Also, because John and Tom are still in the league, all surgeries and medical issues are taken care of by their individual teams. Therefore, there are no medical costs for either player.

BIG BALLER TOM

Big Baller Tom had no medical expenses. He had surgery on his left knee but the team took care of all expenses.

Remaining Income:	$409,302
Medical Expense:	$0

Remaining Income After Medical Expense:	$409,302

STEADY JOHN

Steady John also had no medical expenses. His elbow surgery was paid for by the team.

Remaining Income:	$3,926,294
Medical Expense:	$0

Remaining Income After Medical Expense:	$3,926,294

CHAPTER NINE

MAX PROTECTION

A PLAYBOOK ON INSURANCE

With the Golden State Warriors down by a point, they trust their point guard, Stephen Curry, with the rock; they know he'll make the right decision. With time running out, he dribbles down the right sideline and tries to go baseline. When the Houston Rockets' Patrick Beverley steps up and puts one foot out of bounds to cut off his route, Steph spins to his right, away from Beverley, and takes the circuitous route toward the lane. He spots Andre Iguodala cutting to the basket ahead of James Harden, who is defending him. Now that the defense is out of sorts, lobbing the ball up to Iggy for the alley-oop dunk is a no-brainer. Two points. Golden State's back on top.

To get those two points, Steph had to anticipate that going baseline might not work and have a backup plan. When Beverley stepped up on defense, Plan A couldn't work, but Steph had Plan B already worked out in his head.

So did Iguodala. When the baseline was cut off, Plan B was to spin back the other way and hope that the defense would still be reacting to his first move. They were right. The ploy allowed Iguodala to get a free lane to the basket, and Curry found him. Anticipating what the defense might do and being prepared for it helped the Warriors get the dunk and the lead on that play.

My stepdad always says he suffers from "anticipatory anxiety," which means he prefers to think of things before they happen and turn into a problem. He likes to prepare for the "what ifs." Thinking of the future and preparing for the "what ifs" should be second nature for athletes, because we are constantly trained to anticipate what our opponent is going to do next.

When it comes to insurance, anticipation is a vital skill. No one should spare any expense in protecting himself from the offenses of others, or from simple bad luck. Proper insurance can protect you from the unexpected. Become familiar with insurance, including car, life, property and home, disability, and liability insurance.

CAR INSURANCE

One Sunday in early December 2014, Cam Newton, quarterback of the Carolina Panthers, had one of his best games of the year. He threw three touchdowns and ran for another. He also broke a string of eight consecutive games with an interception and was named Offensive Player of the Week in the Panthers' 41–10 home win over the New Orleans Saints.

After the game, Newton jumped into his Dodge pickup to go home. However, just a few short blocks away from Bank of America Stadium, Cam was unable to avoid a Buick, which was turning into an intersection as he was driving through. The crash resulted in his Dodge flipping and rolling over with him inside. Fortunately, his injuries were minor— if you consider two fractures in his lower back minor. While he missed the following game, he has been fine ever since, so as car accidents go, I think you can call this one minor.

Car insurance is mandatory in the United States, except in New Hampshire. Whether you make a pro athlete's salary or the minimum wage, your income has nothing to do with the requirement to insure your vehicle. Insurance laws are based on the idea that someone who is merely a victim in a crash and not responsible for it shouldn't have to pay out, as it is not fair for someone to suffer a loss, monetary or otherwise, as a result of someone else's negligence. Securing auto insurance is one way to ensure that drivers who may be responsible for an accident are able to pay for damages they have caused.

Of course, there is such a thing as uninsured drivers. Driving without insurance is breaking the law in every state except New Hampshire, but whether you are in an accident with an uninsured driver or are the victim of a hit-and-run, the insurance industry has a way to cover that as well. Insurance companies offer what is called uninsured motorist bodily injury insurance. This will cover any injuries you may have, but will not cover damage to your property. If you do not have this insurance, you could be in for big bills. Twelve U.S. states and Puerto Rico allow insurance companies to offer no-fault insurance, which essentially pays a set amount for your injuries and damages, regardless of who is responsible for the crash.

Car insurance protects you, the car, and other drivers. Younger motorists, like recent college grads or NBA rookies, are forced to pay higher rates because they don't have much driving experience. According to the United States Department of Transportation, 10.4 percent of all fatal car accidents in 2011 involved drivers between twenty-one and twenty-four years old, despite that group's making up only 5 percent of the driving population. There are several coverage options for car insurance shoppers, including property damage, medical payments, collision, comprehensive, towing and rental reimbursement, and bodily injury, but keep in mind: The more expensive the car, the more expensive the insurance.

1. Property Damage: Covers damages to another person's car when you, as an insured driver, cause an accident.

2. Medical Payments: Cover your injuries and those of your passengers, regardless of who caused the crash.

3. Collision: Pays for the damages to any car listed on your policy no matter whose fault the accident was.

4. Comprehensive: Pays for damages to your vehicle that were not caused by an accident but rather by events like fire, theft, or even a rock's cracking your windshield.

5. Towing and Rental Reimbursement: Pays for towing

your car from an accident scene and for the rental car
that you're going to need now that your car is disabled.

6. Bodily Injury: Pays other people's medical bills if they
have injuries from a crash that you caused.

I consider myself a safe driver, but things happen. One
day, I was waiting behind another car at a red light. The light
turned green, I took my foot off the brake, and the car started
slowly rolling forward. I didn't realize that the driver in front
of me must not have seen the light change. He didn't move,
and my car bumped into the back of his, literally at two or
three miles per hour. We both got out of our cars. There was
no damage and the man appeared to be in perfect health. He
looked at me, and I could see his mind working: *Where do I
know this guy from? How do I know this guy . . . the Warriors!*" I
saw the realization wash over his face—and then he suddenly
wanted an ambulance. I knew there was nothing wrong with
him, but he saw me and wanted a big payday. Thankfully,
that little gecko was able to handle it for me!

LIFE INSURANCE

Life insurance is the next important piece of security that you
should have. This insurance is the money paid to your beneficiaries at the time of your death, but it offers many advan-
tages while you are living as well. There are several types of
policies that build equity, or "cash value," that accumulates
over time. This accumulation generally has a guaranteed tax-

deferred growth that allows your money to go untaxed as it is accumulating interest. And when it is taxed later, it will be at a much lower rate. This greatly contributes to the financial security that you're trying to build. That cash value can also be used as collateral to secure a bank loan.

The primary reason people purchase life insurance, though, is for the death benefit. In the event of your untimely demise—even if it occurs in a fiery plane crash or while you're saving small children trapped on a mountainside during an avalanche—a death benefit will pay out money to your family so that they will still receive the income you provided while you were alive.

Unlike car insurance, life insurance is not mandatory. If an athlete is already leaving his family $7 to $8 million, he may decide that the cost of buying life insurance is too expensive and prefer to take that money and invest it in the market. Most of you reading this, however, will need to buy insurance. As with everything, there are benefits and drawbacks to choosing any of the various policies available, so investigate them carefully and consult a financial adviser. A lot of people spend a great deal of time worrying about what kind of car they want to get or how big a house they're going to need, but when it comes to insurance, they'll take any old thing.

No! That's not gonna work!

You have to get what's right for you. Insurance is about protecting what you have. For example, if an athlete hosts a basketball camp, it may seem a safe enough prospect, but if something bad happens, does he have event insurance? Did the kids' parents sign a waiver? If not, this could lead to financial ruin.

What about you? Suppose someone trips on a crack in the sidewalk in front of your house and sues you? Do you have the proper insurance to cover this? Being prepared for the unknown is one of the smartest investments you can make.

PROPERTY AND HOME INSURANCE

Boxer Floyd Mayweather's Las Vegas hideout mansion, tucked away in the middle of the desert, is something to marvel at. There are 24-foot ceilings, crystal chandeliers, and walls covered in red silk and textured glass. The house has a two-story movie theater, and touch-screen video games are built into the kitchen counter. There is also a golf course. The property, which features a 600-square-foot walk-in closet, listed for $3.45 million in 2014. Wouldn't you want to protect that?

For most Americans—pro athletes included—a house is their largest investment, and as such, whether you own a mansion or a small two-bedroom, it represents a significant portion of your wealth. Your home is also where you're the most liable, because the after-cost of a fire or flood, as well as a man-made disaster like burglary or vandalism, could be as high as the entire value of your home. Because of this, it's imperative that you protect yourself with property insurance.

Retired tennis player Chanda Rubin was a perennial Top 20 player during the late 1990s and into the 2000s. She retired in 2006 and has since worked her way onto the United

States Tennis Association's board of directors. A lifelong resident of Louisiana, Rubin built a house in Lafayette. One
night, while asleep during a thunderstorm, she was awak-
ened by the home's alarm system. A little groggy, she went
to see what was going on and discovered smoke coming from
the attic. Chanda got out of the house safely and called 911.
She was the only one home, and no one was hurt. The fire
was apparently started by a lightning strike to her roof. The
house was totaled and everything in it was ruined. She lost
everything.

Rubin may have lost her home and everything in it, but
with home owner's insurance, she was at least monetarily
compensated for her loss. The insurance enabled her to rebuild
on the same land while she lived in a nearby condo. Had she
not had insurance, she would have had to pay out of her own
pocket to rebuild her house and replace her belongings.

If you're not a home owner, you should probably purchase
renters insurance, which most auto insurance companies will
package with your car insurance policy. Renters insurance
basically covers all of your belongings in the event of a burglary or fire. Some renters insurance policies extend to your
car, so if your computer is stolen from your car while you're
in the mall, it's covered.

DISABILITY INSURANCE

During the summer of 2014, at a Team USA scrimmage in
preparation for the FIBA World Cup, Indiana Pacers forward

Paul George, playing for Team Blue, chased down James Harden, who was on the White team. In a very routine play, he swatted at Harden's layup, probably not expecting to block it. But what immediately followed was far from routine: George landed awkwardly and got his foot caught in the stanchion holding up the backboard and basket. As he fell to the ground, his leg snapped mid-shin, resulting in a very bad break. The game was stopped to allow medical personnel to attend to George, but treating the injury became so time-consuming that Team USA officials decided to end the game right there. The immediate speculation was that Paul would not be able to play for at least a year.

Most fans were sad to see Paul George break his leg this way, and Pacers fans found it even more upsetting that he had to sit on the bench in street clothes once the NBA season started. One thing the fans didn't have to worry about was whether or not his income would be affected. As an NBA player with a guaranteed contract, George gets paid whether he is the NBA Finals MVP or injured and not playing for the entire season. You, on the other hand, probably aren't so lucky. Since most companies do not pay employees during the time that they are unable to work due to an injury, purchasing disability insurance is a good idea.

Disability insurance pays you your salary (or a portion of it, depending on the policy you purchase) in the event that you become injured and cannot work. Of course medical insurance covers expenses for treatment of your injury, but if you are not working or bringing in a paycheck, how will you pay for food or utilities? Yes, everyday life must go on even though you are hurt and unable to work. Disability insurance provides for your financial needs and means you'll have one less thing to worry about.

There are various types of disability insurance:

1. Own-Occupation Coverage: This type of policy covers you if you become unable to perform the duties of your own occupation. Even if you can work in another occupation, you would still receive benefits. Of course, this kind of coverage is expensive and insurance companies generally offer these policies only to people who work in relatively risk-free environments.

2. Any-Occupation Coverage: This policy covers you if you become unable to work in any occupation. An any-occupation policy usually has a strict definition of what disability means, and takes into account your earning level, education, and experience.

3. Split Coverage: This is similar to the coverage offered by an own-occupation policy, but after a period of time, usually two years, it becomes an any-occupation policy. This is also known as short-term own-occupation coverage.

4. Residual-Disability Coverage: Residual-disability, also known as income-replacement, policies pay according to the amount of income you have lost due to your injury. For example, if your sickness or injury allows you to work only part-time, whereas you had been previously working full-time, a residual policy will make up the difference in earnings.

Whatever type of coverage you decide is best for you, you will want to be sure that it protects you in the event of illness *or* injury. Some policies cover you only if you are hurt, but not sick, so it is best to get one that covers both. Remember: Insurance policies define sickness as something that comes about only during the time that the policy is in effect. Also, a policy that covers sickness should include mental illness and disabilities related to drugs or alcohol.

LIABILITY INSURANCE

"More drinks! We're running out of drinks at the pool!"

This is not what you want to hear at the annual summer barbecue and pool party that you throw at your house. You jump to it and grab some more liquor from the house. While you're in there, you grab some more of those little umbrellas for the drinks, too. The music is pumping loudly as men and women are diving into the pool, eating the food, and having a good old time. The party is a raging success—until someone slips on the pool deck and breaks his leg. All of a sudden, you become the target of a lawsuit. Do you have an insurance policy to take care of this? Do you have an umbrella policy, which provides an extra layer of protection against the most expensive claims?

Liability insurance covers this kind of incident and can save you a lot of money if something like this were to happen to you. Having a solid liability insurance policy is probably one of the best investments any home owner can make. Opportunists don't care how much money you have—they expect you to have insurance. And if you don't, you could find yourself in a world of financial trouble.

Insurance that protects an individual's home and family, as well as the people who visit, is of great importance—especially for athletes, who are often seen as easy targets for lawsuits. For every asset that needs protection, there is an insurance policy waiting and ready, whether it's to defend your wealth from lawsuits or to protect your beautiful home and the art collection inside.

THE PLAYERS

BIG BALLER TOM

Big Baller Tom did not get property insurance, so when a water pipe burst and flooded his home, he was left to fix everything on his own.

Remaining Income:	$409,302
Cost of Property Replacement:	−$200,000
Income Remaining After Property Damage:	$209,302

STEADY JOHN

Steady John decided to get high-quality property *and* car insurance. When a broken water pipe flooded his house and ruined his floor, furniture, and even some walls, his insurance was there to pay for it.

Remaining Income:	$3,926,294
Insurance Deductible:	−$5,000
Income After Insurance:	$3,921,294

CHAPTER TEN

ENTERING THE ARENA

ESTATE PLANNING

Bobby Phills was a point guard for the Charlotte Hornets back in January 2000. One morning after practice, he was driving home on a curvy, hilly road when he lost control of his 1997 Porsche 993 Cabriolet. It spun around and into the oncoming traffic, where he collided with another car head-on. The driver of the other car emerged with minor injuries, but Phills died instantly. At home, he had a wife and two children waiting. He was only thirty years old, and no one had expected him to die, but no one knows when that day will come.

Young people don't believe they're ever going to die. And I suppose that's fine—as long as they plan for it anyway. Maybe you don't care about what happens to all of your possessions in the event of your death, but you might care about the *people* you leave behind. Setting up a plan for your estate that will protect your family after your demise is very important.

WHAT IS AN ESTATE PLAN?

When we hear the word "estate," we often think of something big. However, your estate is actually a collection of all your worldly possessions, which could be large or small. No matter the size of your property, it is wise that you decide what will happen to it before you are no longer in control of it due to severe illness or death. The best way to do this is by creating a traditional will or a living trust.

A will is a legal document that clearly states how you would like your assets distributed in the event of your demise. You may even appoint guardians for your children. In the absence of a will, the courts will decide where your assets go and who will be raising your children.

It is important to have other things buttoned up as well, because there are instances in which a will can be superseded. For instance, the beneficiary designations on financial accounts take precedence over your will. So, let's say you have a retirement account and you name your husband as the beneficiary, but then you get divorced and marry someone else. Unless you change the beneficiary on your retirement account, your ex-husband will get the money regardless of what's written in your will.

Debt overrides what is written into your will, too. Depending on state law, most debts will be paid by the estate, assuming there are adequate funds. If there are not, then it is the responsibility of the executor—the person the deceased has chosen to handle his estate—to sell off enough property to cover debts. This is the extent of the law concerning debt; it does not become the responsibility of heirs and beneficiaries. You heard me: When someone passes away, his debts are not passed on to his heirs!

You should familiarize yourself with laws concerning inheritance without an estate or will. If you decide not to have a will or estate, your property and wealth will go into probate—legal determination of a will's validity—in which case the government may take a chunk of it. Even if you decide not to leave anything to family and friends, saying so is important so that no one can contest your wishes later. If you want to leave everything to a charity, that too must be spelled out. Simply put, whether you are wealthy or merely middle-class, having an estate plan is essential. Protecting your family and friends, shielding your assets from excessive taxation in probate, and making your last wishes clear are all issues that can be dealt with in an estate plan.

A living trust is commonly implemented by people with significant assets. They may prefer to have this in place in case they become incapacitated, in order to ensure that their business is handled according to their wishes. This document also names an executor.

In selecting an executor, choose someone you trust implicitly, as he or she will make decisions regarding your medical care and other issues specified in your living trust. If you have an illness from which you are expected to recover, it is necessary to specify the duration of the executor's role.

Creating a living trust also saves money and time in court, as an executor would have to be named by a judge if you were to become ill without one. Naming the executor could take a court anywhere from six months to a year to decide, and all the while you'd be incurring legal fees.

IDENTIFY YOUR ASSETS

Your assets include everything of value that you own. You really need to think about everything that you have and determine what is actually worth something and what is not. That baseball glove you wore when you made the diving catch to seal the game and win the 10-and-under championship two decades ago may be of sentimental value to you, but once you're gone, no one is going to want it. Keep this in mind as you make a list of your assets, which is essential in creating a will.

Your list of assets could include:

- Houses
- Vehicles
- Art
- Trophies
- Championship rings

- 401(k) plans
- Pensions
- Deferred compensation
- Investment accounts

IDENTIFY YOUR BENEFICIARIES

Beneficiaries are the people you leave your stuff to. Whoever gets your video game collection would be considered a beneficiary, as would the person who gets your house. While you're young and of sound mind, you need to decide who your beneficiaries are. Obviously, they could include your spouse, kids, mother, sisters, and grandparents, but a lot of athletes leave money to their former school's athletic programs or a charity that helps kids in their hometown. You also need to make decisions about any underage children you may have. Who will be responsible for them? Who will have custody? Who will manage their property until they come of age?

The last thing you want is someone you don't trust taking care of your kids, or your mother, or anyone else you feel responsible for today while you're still alive, earning a living and making your own decisions. The only way you can walk around and not worry about what may happen in the event of your death is to identify the person you want to be in charge of these things and to put that information into your will or trust.

INSTRUCTIONS REGARDING SICKNESS AND DEATH

An estate or living trust for the most part covers your belongings and what will become of them—but what will become of you? Suppose you are sick and unable to make decisions regarding your own health? Estate plans are usually accompanied by a health care directive, which alerts everyone as to what your wishes are in the event that you become fatally ill. A health care directive is a legal document and as such must be followed by doctors and family. It can let them know whether or not you want to be kept alive by a feeding tube, or if you want to donate your organs. It can even give instructions regarding funeral arrangements.

TIPS

1. Talk to an estate lawyer about creating an estate plan.
2. Determine whether or not you should have a living trust.
3. Write down all of your assets, so you are clear about what you will leave behind.
4. If you have children, give some thought as to who will take care of them.
5. Identify a friend to dispose of unwanted items.
6. Create a health care directive.
7. Leave directions about funeral arrangements.

Having an estate plan is very important for the people you leave behind.

THE PLAYERS

BIG BALLER TOM

Tom doesn't have an estate plan. He doesn't want to think about death and dying. However, if he were to die now, there wouldn't be much to fight over, as his income is dwindling fast. So, for the purpose of this exercise, the cost of the fight that would have taken place, had there been something to fight over, will be kept at $0.

Remaining Income:	$209,302
Estate Setup Costs:	$0
Income After Estate Expenses:	$209,302

STEADY JOHN

Steady John set up a living trust, which will protect his family and ensure that his wife and child are cared for in the event of his incapacitation or death.

Remaining Income:	$3,921,294
Estate Setup Costs:	−$5,000
Income After Estate Expenses:	$3,916,294

CHAPTER ELEVEN

PLAYING YOUR POSITION

FINDING A JOB IN THE FIELD

I remember playing in my first NBA game. I was ecstatic. Wide-eyed, I looked around the arena. Sure, I had played in arenas and in front of big crowds before, but this was different—this was the NBA. It didn't matter how many minutes I got, or how well I did. All that mattered was that I was in uniform on an NBA floor.

The game itself wasn't that exciting, especially since I didn't play that much. I was able to enjoy it from a seat on the bench, sitting and watching just like the fans who had bought tickets. Afterward, I saw my stepparents and ran over to talk to them about what had transpired over the last two and a half hours. There were some congratulations and a few questions, but then, seemingly out of nowhere, my stepdad asked, "What are you going to do after your career is over?"

I had just played my first NBA game. What was he talking about?

"What are you going to do when your NBA career is over?" he said again.

I came back down to earth as I realized that this was how he was getting me ready for a post-NBA career. He wanted me to understand that this basketball life is a short one and could be gone at any time, so I have to constantly be preparing for the next step.

The average length of a basketball player's career is 4.8 years. That means an athlete's career in professional sports could be over by the time he is twenty-five or -six. Professional athletes either retire voluntarily, suffer a career-ending injury, or fail to have their contract renewed, but one way or another, sooner or later the game will leave them, whether they want it to or not. That means preparation for a second career is paramount. Even if athletes have enough money, they can go insane golfing and lounging around the house all day after having had a busy playing career. This is one of the few unfortunate aspects of being a professional athlete. In almost any other career—doctor . . . lawyer . . . accountant— the job can last an entire lifetime, but a professional athlete's job lasts just a handful of years.

Athletes should be thinking about a second career while they are still playing. Start thinking about what else you're good at; take an assessment test and figure out what you like. Websites such as www.self-directed-search.com and www.mynextmove.org can help in this process. If an NBA player needs a college degree for his dream job, he can get it done in the summer. And there are opportunities to do course work online.

If you plan on staying in sports, talk to people already doing the job that you want to shoot for. There are athletic trainers, financial consultants, strength and conditioning coaches, general managers, coaches, assistant coaches, scouts, broadcasters, etc. Professional basketball players can visit the NBA office and talk to the commissioner, or go to the union offices to meet with the leadership there. Being a professional athlete can open doors that could be useful later in life. The union will support your search for your next career. The NBPA provides:

- Summer School for Broadcasting
- Continuing Education
- A Coaching Program
- General Manager Training

One thing my stepdad constantly talks about is finding your comparative advantage. After playing basketball for their entire lives, NBA players have a comparative advantage over others in basketball knowledge. Therefore, finding a job in the field of basketball is often easier for them than doing something completely new. If you want to preserve your comparative advantage, there are many jobs in professional basketball you could investigate now for when your playing career is over.

For those who have never been professional players, there are still ways to obtain jobs in sports. Sports industry jobs are often targeted by collegiate athletes who never played at the professional level, as well as by those entering the workforce who grew up as big sports fans. Either way, people looking for sports jobs are usually already interested in sports, and thus have their own comparative advantage over others.

Here is a list of a few opportunities:

COACHING

When it comes to coaching, there's not really a shortage of available spots. All teams have several types of coaches. Every NBA team has a head coach and three assistants, and there are also job opportunities in the NBA Development League (NBDL), the NCAA, and high schools. Most jobs are filled through references, and in sports it's no different. If you are not a pro athlete, you probably did not play on your college team, but where you went to school is a good place to start looking. You can probably go right to the coach in his office to explain what your intentions are, cutting out any middle-men. For players, starting at the school where you played or contacting your coach if he has gone on to another school is a smart move. Hopefully, you left your university with a good reputation within the athletic department and around campus.

The NBPA has a program that brings current NBA players to coach at the Top 100 Camp for the best high school basketball players, which it holds every year. The camp gives pro players firsthand experience in scouting, drawing up Xs and Os, and theory. Taking advantage of this camp can teach you some things about coaching and lets people around the league know that you're serious about it.

You shouldn't just play the game, but should learn how to think about it at the same time. That's a major part of coaching. Athletes have a unique opportunity to master the game, because they can learn while they're playing; it's kind of like on-the-job-training. Also, talk to your current coach. Head coaches bring in their former players as assistants all the time. This is mainly because they realize that this player will know the coach's plays, schemes, and attitude and will be able to reinforce the things they are trying to teach their current players.

SCOUTING

Scouting can be a great opportunity for retired players, but they have to love to travel. Some teams' scouting departments consist of as many as ten people, so there are many jobs in scouting. Here are a few:

GAME SCOUT

The responsibility of a game scout is to travel to other cities to watch other teams and send back comprehensive play sets and other pertinent information that can help the head coach build a game strategy to play against them. This is a position the head coach really relies on. Game scouts typically travel to several games a week.

COLLEGE SCOUT

College scouts watch hundreds of college games a year, evaluating talent and building a database for the NBA Draft. The amount of research done on potential draft picks seems to increase every season, so you have to really be prepared to crunch some numbers.

INTERNATIONAL SCOUT

An international scout travels all over the world, keeping a database of worthy players who may become available for the NBA Draft.

DIRECTOR OF PLAYER DEVELOPMENT

The main duty here is to help younger players adjust to the league and the long season, to learn the playbook, and in many cases, to grow into adulthood. This is one of the most political positions in the NBA: The director of player development works for the team, but he reports to and is instructed by the NBA. The team's general manager can also assign him other responsibilities. At the same time, the person in this role is expected to represent the interests of the players, so he has to win their trust in order to truly be able to help them.

Once I took this position with the Orlando Magic, it didn't take long for the players to see me as a "suit." To them,

I had become part of management, and they weren't sure that I could be trusted anymore. This was despite the fact that I had spent the last three years as a player on the team, right up until I'd blown out my knee a few months before.

This job depends on your respecting the players and vice versa. If an athlete is thinking about becoming a director of player development, he has got to lay the groundwork early to establish trust and mutual respect with his fellow players. There is usually one director of player development per team, and retired players often take on the job. Teams usually have another position called director of player services, whose job is to oversee the handling of the players' off-court but team-related needs—such as passports, driver's licenses, attorneys, insurance, family matters, and ticket requests.

GENERAL MANAGER OR PRESIDENT OF BASKETBALL OPERATIONS

Some teams split the general manager position into two. The president of basketball operations runs the day-to-day activities of the department and he may also supervise the general manager. However, in many organizations one person holds both positions. Basketball operations entail supervising the equipment manager, secretary, athletic trainer, strength and conditioning coach, physical therapist, director of player development, director of player services, head and assistant coaches, scouting department, and the team's most important position, general manager. The GM decides which players to bring in through the draft, which players to trade away from the team, and what to get in return. For all intents and purposes, the GM is the face of the organization.

COMMUNITY AMBASSADOR

Some teams around the league wanted former players to stay connected with the fans, so they created a program called Community Ambassadors. The teams use retired players to work in their community relations department and be a presence at various events around their city. They are the face of the team's work in the community. During the course of the year, they may make several hundred appearances at camps, schools, and charitable events.

EXECUTIVE DIRECTOR, NATIONAL BASKETBALL PLAYERS ASSOCIATION

If an athlete is an ambitious person who has paid attention to league politics and attended union meetings, he could apply for this position. The players' union is a multifaceted organization. To lead it, one must have a background in law and contracts as well as an eclectic array of skills, including the ability to understand and communicate the players' perspective. Similarly, one could try to become part of the management team of the National Basketball Retired Players Association (NBRPA).

COLOR COMMENTATOR

Many retired players flock to television and radio gigs to do the color commentator job, but not many of them last, because they haven't studied it as an art form. The opportunities for commentating are numerous—each team has at least three people covering games on TV and two on radio—so there is the potential for at least two color commentators per team. There are national color analysts like Charles Barkley, Chris Webber, Kenny Smith, Greg Anthony, Shaquille O'Neal, and others. You don't have to be a superstar—players like Tim Legler, Tom Tolbert, Steve Kerr, Bruce Bowen, and many others have made a living in the media and are respected as members of the press. Then there are local, in-studio commentators, and finally, analysts who cover everything.

And there's more good news for would-be commentators: The NBPA has developed a relationship with Syracuse University, which has one of the best communications departments in the country. Each year it holds a two-week program in which players learn the tricks of the trade and leave with actual footage of themselves covering a game.

You should also keep your career plans in mind all those times you get interviewed by reporters. It's a good idea not only to talk to them about their jobs but to develop relationships with them so they can help you later when you're making that post-NBA transition. There is absolutely nothing wrong with talking to an expert in the field you want to go into, and when you're a player on an NBA team, everyone is willing to talk to you.

This is an area where nonathletes can easily get in. The majority of play-by-play announcers never played the game—in fact, I can't think of one offhand. Many of them did it in college for the school's TV or radio station and have been practicing their craft and honing their skills for years.

REFEREE

A few players have decided to become something they oftentimes hate: a referee. This is a tough gig, because not only is it physical night in and night out but there is a lot of training involved, and you have to learn rules of the game that you thought you already knew. Also, it's very difficult to break into refereeing, for you're competing with people who have been doing it for years. Still, Haywoode Workman and Leon Wood are two prominent ex-players who now wear a whistle around their necks. Once you're in and show your competency, you can be part of this profession for many years. One downside for former players who become referees is that they can no longer fraternize with many of their former peers in the league. Once ex-teammates become coaches, GMs, and team officials, those relationships unfortunately must change.

Obviously, you don't have to have been a player to get into refereeing, but it is a field in which the more experience you have, the better off you'll be. If you start out by getting certified at a lower level, like high school, you can work your way up through the world of officiating.

ATHLETIC DIRECTOR

The role of the athletic director (AD) can be described as a "medicine router." For many teams, the AD is required to manage all the doctors the team uses. Teams use a lot of outside specialists, and ADs are required to coordinate with all of them on behalf of the players. They manage appointments, find the best specialists in the field, bring them to games, arrange physicals, and set up standard therapeutic work. Whether you played the game or not, having some background in medicine and management wouldn't hurt here.

If athletes know their sport well enough, they can stick around and have a postplaying career doing one of the jobs described above. But it's not just about knowledge. Players should also treat people in their organization well and build strong relationships that create goodwill and can help them when they aren't playing anymore and need guidance making that next move. The flip side is that earning a bad reputation, even in just one city, can sometimes follow a player for years—or decades. So don't be a diva or think you're better than anyone else in the organization.

You must protect your image because, in many cases, your image can precede you. The NBA is a small community, and someone you'd never even think of could end up having a say in whether or not you get a job somewhere down the road, either during your playing career or afterward. This worked out nicely when John Gabriel, then-GM of the Orlando Magic, hired former Philadelphia 76ers star Julius Erving to work in the Magic front office. Gabriel started off as a film coordinator with the 76ers during Erving's playing days, and never forgot the encouragement Dr. J had given him.

Conversely, over the years, I've seen how many ex-athletes are haunted by their bad reputations. Most of them are never hired. Understanding your individual reputation—and protecting it—is of extreme importance, so act accordingly on the court, at the practice facility, while being interviewed, and on social media. In other words, don't post anything on Facebook, Twitter, Instagram, Tumblr, or anywhere else that you may regret later. This may sound silly, but it may actually be a good idea to count to ten before hitting a button to post anything. In those ten seconds, think about whether or not that post will be negatively perceived by anyone. You also should not give control of your Facebook page or Twitter account to anyone. Just as you need to sign every check you write, you need to see every post that goes up.

Owning your name as a domain on the Web is as important as not giving control to someone else. You don't want anyone setting up a website with your name and putting whatever he wants on it. Using a company like GoDaddy to obtain ownership of your name is a good idea. If your name is John Douglas Smith, get the domain name for johnsmith, johndsmith, johndouglassmith, etc. Some people will try to use your name by altering the spelling by one letter and then lead the public to believe it is really you. At the end of the day, if athletes don't protect their brand while they're playing, nobody is going to give them a job when they're not.

Critics might say that thinking about a second career could dissipate a player's focus while he is still in the league, but that is not true. In fact, while they're playing, most NBAers are proficient in things besides basketball (e.g., acting, music, or a variety of other pursuits)—but these same athletes are unsure of what they want to do once their careers are over. Thinking about a second career is no different. You never know when you'll play your last game in the NBA, so preparation is very important.

TIPS

1. Start thinking about a second career early. This is important so that you can figure out what it is that you like and want to do.
2. Talk to people who are doing the job you feel you may want to pursue. Find out what their duties are and how they handle them.
3. Consult with the league and union officials about your intentions.
4. Take advantage of opportunities offered by the union, such as the coaching camp.
5. Begin networking with current and former coaches.
6. Contact your college athletic director.

7. Protect your image. Be nice to people. You never know who may be responsible for hiring you later.

THE PLAYERS

BIG BALLER TOM

Big Baller Tom hasn't built such a good reputation. He has a lot of charisma and may want to be a broadcaster, but he hasn't done much about it. Only time will tell how it works out for him.

Remaining Income:	$209,302
Education Expenses:	$0
Total Income After Education:	$209,302

STEADY JOHN

Steady John finished up his college degree and graduated with a BA in sociology. He's built a good reputation around the NBA, and his teammates respect him. One of the assistant GMs on his team has talked to him about what it's like to work in a front office, and his coaches think he might make a good coach someday. He's taken a class in public speaking and has begun to pursue a master's degree in business (MBA). Someone from ESPN has already approached him about doing some broadcasting if his team doesn't make the playoffs this year. John would probably like to be a GM, but isn't sure yet. Either way, all options will be available to him.

Remaining Income:	$3,916,294
Education Expenses:	−$100,000
Total Income after Education:	$3,816,294

THE PLAYERS: CONCLUSION

Steady John and Big Baller Tom demonstrate, in a crude way, what happens when athletes don't pay close attention to their finances. In the case of Steady John, his choices—although expensive at times—save him a great deal in the long run. He invested in his education, insurance, and an estate plan, and paid all his taxes, so despite his expenses, he is still holding on to $3,816,294 of his salary. After three years in the league, he is now poised to get a second contract, and the discipline he developed during his rookie deal ensures that he is on track toward a healthy financial career.

Big Baller Tom, on the other hand, made plenty of mistakes during the first three years of his career. Tom had kids out of wedlock and is paying child support. He overspent on luxury goods and supported a big entourage. All of these issues, in addition to the fact that he refused to sign a prenup or create an estate plan, have put Tom on a shaky foundation. Although he is in an incredibly precarious situation, with his next multimillion-dollar contract he has an opportunity to not only climb out of the financial hole he has dug for himself but also to become financially solvent. The choice is up to him, just as it is to all athletes.

CHAPTER TWELVE

DO NOT FOUL OUT OF THE GAME

HOW TO AVOID COMMON MONEY MISTAKES

In May 1997, the NBA Western Conference semifinals were into the fifth game of the series. The Los Angeles Lakers and the Utah Jazz were tied with ten seconds left in the game. The purple and gold were led by Shaquille O'Neal and point guard Nick Van Exel, but at this crucial point of the game, they elected to have rookie Kobe Bryant, who had graduated from high school less than a year before, bring the ball up the length of the court. Bryant got upcourt, took a few dribbles, and then fired up a three-pointer to win the game. Sounds nice, except that Kobe's shot fell short. Way short. In fact, it was an air ball. The crowd went out of control as they saw the prior year's overall No. 13 pick in the draft fail so miserably.

But it wasn't over. The game continued into overtime, and in the final minute, Van Exel swung the ball around to Kobe, who again tossed up a ball that didn't even reach the rim. The Lakers dug in, played defense, got the ball back, and once more put it in the hands of their rookie, who shot his third air ball. Kobe's fourth and final air ball came with just six seconds remaining in overtime. The Lakers lost that game, and the series.

We all know that Kobe has gone on to become one of the top NBA players of all time. He also went on to ultimately lead his team to five championships, including three consecutive titles, and he once scored 81 points in a game, second only to the 100 points that Wilt Chamberlain dropped one night in Hershey, Pennsylvania. In addition, he won gold medals in the 2008 and 2012 Olympics.

Kobe's career is an example of how mistakes are correctable with hard work. His inexperience on the basketball court can be compared to a lack of financial knowledge, which can lead to rookie mistakes. Here are the most common money mistakes.

COMMON MONEY MANAGEMENT MISTAKES

NOT PROTECTING YOUR ASSETS

A significant number of NBA players have an entourage. Sometimes, they're friends who fulfill legitimate roles.

Early in my career I had a teammate—we'll call him Joe—who brought his childhood friend Brian along with him when he first got into the league. The two had grown up together, and now Joe was making money and in a position to help his friend out by giving him a job as his assistant. Brian was actually qualified to do it: He had graduated from college with a degree in business administration and knew about finance. Based on that, it only made sense that he was put in charge of paying a few bills, in addition to some other duties.

Joe had another employee as well. Bobby was sort of an assistant to the assistant. To figure out how that makes sense, you'd have to ask them, but that's the setup they had. Both of the employees had credit cards from one of Joe's accounts. So, when out of the blue Joe got a call from his bank alerting him that his account was overdrawn, he immediately called Brian to see what was going on. They discovered that Bobby had been using the credit card at his leisure, buying clothes, purchasing gifts for his girlfriend, and gassing up his car. Brian, unaware of Bobby's dealings, had been paying the credit card bills out of the account that was now overdrawn.

After becoming aware of the credit card misuse, Joe wanted to be sure that he was only being robbed of money. He smartly brought in an auditor. Once they started reviewing the books, it was revealed that while Bobby was getting jiggy with the credit card, Brian was writing unauthorized checks.

Joe couldn't believe it. It was a painful lesson to be reminded that there is no shortage of people who, if given the opportunity, will steal from you. He had known Brian since they were kids; this was someone he had trusted. Of course, Joe fired both him and Bobby.

To avoid theft, consistently review your bank statement,

credit card balances, and any other accounts that you have money flowing through. These regular check-ins will allow you to notice discrepancies right away.

Robert Swift, a 2004 NBA lottery pick, was drafted right out of high school. He played just five years and was out of the league by the time he was twenty-three. Despite playing for such a short time, he earned more than $11 million during his NBA career. Yet he ended up broke. According to his high school coach, Gino Lacava, his parents' "fatal greed" was responsible for his downfall. The coach claimed that Swift's parents "became hypnotized by the $4.4 million" the Seattle Supersonics gave their then-eighteen-year-old son. After he suffered an anterior cruciate ligament (ACL) tear, Swift saw his career fade before he could gain financial stability.

Had Swift been 100 percent involved in his finances, he could have taken control of the situation before it got out of hand.

POOR CREDIT DECISIONS

Establishing credit and protecting your credit rating is important in growing your wealth. Your credit score is what banks and other financial institutions use to determine their likelihood of getting their money back if they grant you a home loan or finance your start-up business. They look at your history of paying debts like credit cards or car loans to see if you pay bills on time, or at all. They also want to see if you have ever declared bankruptcy.

Your credit score, also known as a FICO score, is based

on a credit-scoring model created by the Fair Isaac Corporation. It is the magic number by which financial decisions
regarding you are determined. Based on the information in
your credit report, the FICO model comes up with a single
number that represents your entire life's credit history. This
number can be anywhere from 300 to 850. A rating above
700 is generally considered a good score. The higher your
score, the lower the interest rate, and vice versa.

Your creditworthiness affects the rate you will have to
pay for your car insurance. It impacts the interest rates you
pay for credit cards and any loans. Essentially, having bad
credit will cost you money. Delinquency in paying bills or
letting your student loan go into default will lower your
credit rating, causing you to be charged more money to borrow money. You may borrow money to buy a house or car,
or just to use a credit card. If you are paying for all of these
privileges at a high interest rate, they can really add up to a
lot of money that you would not have had to pay, had you
paid your credit card on time.

It's best to establish credit while you're young, because it's
easier than when you're older—oddly, financial institutions
are suspicious of mature individuals who haven't established
any form of credit, and thus are reluctant to trust them. Young
people typically do not have credit histories, and banks will
gladly allow them the chance to establish credit by offering
one of their credit cards or a car loan.

I know several people from college who got suckered into
getting a high-interest credit card, which banks offer to students all the time. They'll tell you that it is a good way to

establish good credit, and it is, if you can afford it. If you can't afford it, or if you don't have the discipline to not overspend, then any credit card at this time is a bad idea. Yet student after student signs up for these cards, unaware of the consequences until they blow them out—they stretch the cards beyond their limits and have no way to make the payments. If you don't pay the bill, the card will be canceled and your credit will be shot. The upside is that a negative history is usually wiped from your credit in seven years.

Banks regularly have credit card promotions for recent college grads and current students. While you have to be careful about which credit card or car loan you choose, this is the chance to establish good credit right from the get-go. Just remember, it will be to your advantage to pay all of your bills on time, not on the last day of the grace period. Expenses such as a cell phone or a cable bill won't necessarily help build your credit, but not paying those bills can negatively impact it. Putting as many bills as possible on auto-pay is an easy way to make sure they get paid on time. Auto-pay is an excellent tool for people who travel extensively, such as sports professionals: One day we need to be in Detroit, Milwaukee the next, and then Salt Lake City two days after that.

Once credit is established, protecting it becomes the new focus. Protecting your credit means regularly monitoring your credit report to make sure no one has opened a line of credit in your name or that no negative information is being reported in error. To get a free copy of your credit report each year, a good website is annualcreditreport.com.

Identity theft is nothing to play with. Once someone steals

your identity, it can take several years and thousands of dollars to straighten everything out. A paper shredder is a great investment. Shred any papers that contain personal data, such as bank information or your social security number.

FRIENDS AND MONEY

If you want to keep a friend, my advice to you is not to allow money matters to enter the friendship. In short, keep your money on the right and your friends on the left!

Let's say that you have a decent salary, but are not yet at the point where you can buy a condo on Park Avenue. It'll take a few more years and pay raises to put you in a position to do that. However, to your friends you may look as if you are doing really well because you make more than they do. They may even ask to borrow money. There are two problems here. First, your friends are likely to ask to borrow an amount of money that they can't afford to pay back. Second, you more than likely can't afford to lend them the money. You understand just how tight your money is, but your friends don't. Before you lend money to anyone, you should determine whether or not you can afford to lose that money. If you can, then go ahead and lend it. If you can't, then don't.

One of your friends may take things a step further and ask you to cosign for a car loan. This is not a good idea at all. Do not cosign for anything for anyone. More often than not, it turns out badly. If your friend hasn't taken the time or care to straighten out his own credit, then what makes you think he'll protect yours? If you cosign for someone because his credit isn't strong enough to obtain that loan on his own, and subsequently he misses or is late with payments, it affects your credit. Then, when you go to buy a car or something, you could end up paying a higher interest rate than you would have—or worse, get declined.

For athletes, this is an even bigger issue. Many businessmen assume that professional athletes are very rich and extremely stupid. They also believe that we don't have to take investing seriously because if a project fails, it won't necessarily impact our lifestyle. Over the years, I have been asked to invest in movie productions, energy drinks, several restaurants, nightclubs, cultural programs, and clothing lines. I seriously considered some of them, but my financial team was always there to properly advise me.

An athlete may think that by investing in a friend's business idea, he is helping his friend. But if that friend doesn't have a track record of starting up businesses successfully or at least running the kind of business he is trying to start, the chances are pretty good that this investment is a bad idea.

All too often these business proposals are schemes to get your money. Many times, my stepfather was approached by associates, or maybe folks he knew in passing, who were pushing money schemes they claimed would make us rich. These people would go through him in the belief that this was the best way to convince me of the worthiness of their claims.

Even an acquaintance with honest intentions will approach you with, say, an idea for a website, or an app. Sure, you may want to show some interest because it's your friend, but at the end of the day, even his proposal should be pushed off to your financial adviser to determine its worthiness. If it's a bad egg and you have no business putting eight cents, let alone $8 million, into it, your adviser will let your friend know that it's a no-go. That way, you don't have to worry about feeling guilty or alienating a buddy.

San Francisco Giants pitcher Barry Zito sued his friend Michael Clark over a $3 million investment. Zito claimed that his friend tricked him into investing in a company called dotFIT that was marketing a software program promoting holistic health and fitness to health clubs worldwide. It was supposed to raise $20 million in equity, but according to Zito's court filing, dotFIT instead used his money to pay high salaries and bonuses to its employees.

An athlete may also involve his family in a business in order for them to make money independently, instead of having to dip into the athlete's pocket. But, just as with friends who want the athlete to invest in a business, a company with the sole intention of providing something to family members will be a success only if they know something about running a business.

Ryan Howard of the Philadelphia Phillies started a company called RJH Enterprises just after the 2006 season. His father, Ron, was named as the business manager; his mother, Cheryl, was chief financial officer; his brother Chris was general counsel; and his twin brother, Corey, became his personal assistant, moving to Philly and living in Ryan's house there.

RJH was supposed to secure marketing opportunities for Ryan, but in the several years the company was in existence, none was secured. Then, in 2011, when Ryan wanted to shift his marketing management to his agent at Creative Artists Agency, a major player in the entertainment industry, and dissolve RJH, Corey filed a lawsuit. He was upset that there would be no more company. Corey had been getting paid $7,972 every two weeks by his brother. Their father was upset about the dissolution, too, and wanted $5 million each for him and Cheryl.

Ryan filed a countersuit that claimed his mother, as CFO, had authorized payments to family members totaling $2,795,337.38. The case was settled in 2014 for an undisclosed amount, but it left the once-close family fractured, strongly suggesting yet again that the only way to maintain friendships and familial relationships is to not mix money with friends or family.

BAD PERSONAL BUSINESS INVESTMENTS

In addition to having too much faith in investing in friends and family, often athletes themselves will make poor business investments. In fact, bad investments are one of the most common reasons athletes lose their fortunes.

"It was a real estate proposal," recalls former NBA player Bobby Jackson. "The business wasn't ridiculous, but this guy wanted me to invest two and a half million dollars in it. I actually thought about it, but my financial team looked at the plan and thought it was way too risky. My financial team really saved me, because those guys eventually went bankrupt and lost the business."

As a former professional athlete, I can say that I'm repeatedly approached with "sensational" plans to make money. The snake-oil vendors typically say that it's the best potion or whatever and that nobody ever thought of it before, and that all they need is a few hundred thousand dollars to get started. We are frequently pitched to start up the next great restaurant, the next superhealthy energy drink, or the next comfy line of T-shirts. Players often get suckered into investing without any real knowledge of specifics. Some financial consultant will suggest it to the athlete, and he'll believe that this is what will propel him to Warren Buffett status.

In a scandal that began in 2008, over the course of two years Wall Street broker Jeffrey Rubin of Lighthouse Point, Florida, convinced thirty-one top-tier National Football League (NFL) players, including Plaxico Burress, Santonio Holmes, Javon Kearse, Santana Moss, Kyle Orton, Terrell Owens, Clinton Portis, and Fred Taylor, to invest in a casino in Alabama. Collectively, they put in around $40 million; however, by 2010, Alabama's gambling task force pressured the Country Crossing Casino to shut down, as its developer, Ronnie Gilley, pleaded guilty to offering bribes to legislators. None of the players was able to recoup any of his losses, which averaged nearly $1.4 million per athlete.

According to Brad Bennett, the executive vice president and chief of enforcement for the Financial Industry Regulatory Authority (FINRA), "This case demonstrates how broker misconduct can target high-income, inexperienced, and vulnerable investors. Jeffrey Rubin took advantage of professional athletes who placed their trust in him."

This was ironic, considering that the reason Rubin was viewed positively by the NFL community was that he exposed a Ponzi scheme conducted by former NFL agent William "Tank" Black. They thought Rubin was someone they could trust. But he didn't just fool these players; he fooled their investment advisers. In fact, Rubin first got in trouble for this scam back in 2012, when Owens, in a *Gentlemen's Quarterly* interview, blasted the financial advisers who had told him to invest $2 million with Rubin. However, it wasn't until 2013 that FINRA finally barred Rubin from the securities industry, after he made four "unsuitably risky" investment recommendations to retired Baltimore Ravens player Samari Rolle, who lost $3 million on the deals.

To be clear, these players did not get their money back just because they caught this guy. If the perpetrator of a scam is unable to pay the money back, the victim has limited recourse. A court can only tell you that a person is obligated to pay you; it does not actually make the person pay. To collect money from a person who can't pay, you would have to get the sheriff to garnish his wages or put a lien on any assets he may have, such as his house. But if you're dealing with someone who has no payroll job and doesn't own any assets, he would be considered judgment-proof and you'd be hard-pressed to find a lawyer who would want to take the case—after all, the lawyer has to get paid, too. In a case like the Jeffrey Rubin scam, it is very unlikely that the victims will get back any of their $1.4 million each.

Athletes try to start businesses by investing boatloads of

money into them instead of maybe starting a small business and allowing it to grow organically as they and their employees learn the particulars of running that kind of company. Often athletes who believe they are sitting on a big pile of money will attempt to start a record company or a clothing line. However, the reality is they don't know any more about running a record company than they do about building a rocket to go to the moon. This means they'll need to hire personnel to run the company while they're traveling all over the country with their team. Who has time to check up on the day-to-day activities of a record company? You need to invest wisely by doing a little research before you put money into a company. Try investing in something that you know about, something that you're interested in.

You don't have to look very hard to find examples of former athletes losing big money because of bad business investments. Derrick Coleman, who was drafted with the very first pick in the 1990 draft by the New Jersey Nets, invested in a Detroit mall called Coleman's Corner. Although his intentions were to help revitalize the city he grew up in by creating business opportunities and jobs, investing in a shopping mall in one of the city's most downtrodden areas was not a good idea.

The four-store strip mall, which Coleman sank six million of his own dollars into, represented the first retail center to open on Detroit's Linwood Street since it had been decimated by riots all the way back in 1967. One of the businesses in the mall was a pizza place owned by Coleman and managed by a childhood friend. As the economy started to slide, the pizza place began to falter, and as Coleman was losing money with the strip mall, he was also losing the money he had put into the pizza business.

Former Olympic gold medal skater Dorothy Hamill was living the life. After becoming America's Sweetheart at age nineteen during the 1976 Olympics, she was given a million-dollar-a-year contract to skate on prime-time television. Recognized on the street by her short hairstyle, she was able in the '80s to overcome a years-long battle with depression. In 1991, she married her second husband, and later that year the two of them purchased the Ice Capades, which had gone bankrupt the year before. (Purchasing this large, bankrupt company already sounds like a bad idea.) She bought it at a liquidation sale, acquiring a warehouse full of costumes and ice machines and, most important, the name. However, she had to borrow millions just to keep the business afloat, before selling it three years later. This ultimately led to her bankruptcy in 1996.

In one big-money scheme, over the course of five years beginning in 2006, a Venezuelan businessman named Claudio Osorio swindled several investors—including NBA players Dwight Howard, Carlos Boozer, Alonzo Mourning, and Howard Eisley—out of $40 million when they backed his company, InnoVida Holdings, Inc., which was supposed to develop free housing for underserved communities. The project never broke ground, but as it languished, Osorio moved all of the investment money to offshore accounts in the Cayman Islands, making the money harder to trace.

In 2013, Osorio was sentenced to more than twelve years in jail and ordered to pay between $20 and $50 million to his investors. As Osorio serves out his sentence, it doesn't appear likely that his victims will get their money back, partially due to a parallel bankruptcy filing. Attorney Mark Meland, the bankruptcy trustee for InnoVida, claims that the money from the Cayman Islands can't be recovered because it was spent on Osorio's "extravagant lifestyle." Before going to prison he entertained high-profile politicians like Bill and Hillary Clinton and Barack Obama at fund-raisers he would throw at his home on swank Cayman Brac.

In order to look legitimate, Osorio had several high-profile figures on his board of directors, including former Florida governor Jeb Bush, whose name would, of course, attract big investors. This company even stole more than $10 million in federal funding. According to the *Miami Herald*, Osorio and his wife "threw dazzling parties, contributed large sums to charities, and flashed fat financial portfolios to give the appearance that they were as rich and sophisticated as the celebrities, financial moguls, and business people with whom they rubbed elbows."

Incidents like this are a perfect example of the way money-losing deals and even outright scams can come in an attractive package. Anytime you are considering investing in anything, it is important to investigate the company and all of the people involved as thoroughly as you can. When a deal sounds too good to be true, chances are it is.

These situations demonstrate the extent to which people are at risk of being scammed out of everything they have saved. That's why it's so important to pay attention to your money and recognize that not every proposal is worthwhile or legitimate. It's important to know that if people are going to offer you a once-in-a-lifetime opportunity, it probably has nothing to do with you. They just want to use someone's money other than their own. If the money is lost and the business fails, then you take the financial hit.

LACKING STOCK MARKET EXPERTISE

Rather than investing in a conservative portfolio with a steady rate of return, most investors, whether they are high earners or not, think they need to make more money and invest in shaky stocks with a high rate of return. The problem is that this is too risky—these stocks come crashing down all the time. Unless you're watching your investments daily and buying and selling every day, this is not the way to go. Especially if you have twenty years or more to let your investment portfolio grow, you should absolutely steer clear of companies that you think will produce a high rate of return right away.

Recently, we've seen two major stock reversals. In the early 2000s, the tech-stock balloon of the '90s came back down to earth and brought a lot of investors' bottom lines with it. Then there were the financial stocks in 2008. When they lost value, things got so bad that it sent the entire country into a recession.

RELINQUISHING YOUR POWER OF ATTORNEY

Handing over full authority to someone to write checks, transfer money, pay bills, and do a host of other tasks on your behalf, without obtaining your permission, is granting that person "power of attorney." If you give someone power of attorney over your money and belongings, he or she can legally make financial decisions that could cause you to go bankrupt. This is never a good idea unless you become physically or mentally incapacitated.

In 1984, Muhammad Ali was diagnosed with Parkinson's disease, which, in addition to creating physical symptoms, can cause confusion and dementia. His wife, Yolanda Williams, retains power of attorney and is in control of his fortune. In Ali's case, giving power of attorney to his wife was critical.

At the onset of a debilitating disease, you may want to consider planning for your care and ultimate demise ahead of time. Otherwise, the court will decide who will retain control over your assets. If this happens, not only will you likely have to pay this person (whereas a friend or relative rarely asks to be paid) but there is a good chance the court will assign someone you would not have picked.

There are two types of powers of attorney: general and specific (also called limited). A general power of attorney is unlimited in scope and duration, and permits the selected executor to act as your legal representative in relation to financial matters until such time as it is revoked. In other words, that person has complete control of your finances until you formally terminate the agreement. In contrast, a specific power of attorney imposes limits upon the named representative, and may restrict the scope of that person's powers to a single type of action or a single transaction. For example, you can give your tax consultant the power to fight an IRS audit for you, or you can give your personal assistant the power to set up a camp for kids that you're going to run in the summer.

Granting power of attorney is dangerous, because it makes it extremely difficult to track how your money is being spent. Giving someone that much power over your wealth creates temptation. If you find yourself in a predicament where you need an executor, do not assign general—i.e., unlimited—power of attorney. You should think only in terms of limited power of attorney, and it should be on very specific terms that clearly define the duration and scope of your representative's powers. I suggest you do it with the help of a lawyer and put it in writing.

RETIREMENT

The best time to begin saving for retirement is upon the first day of your first job, but not many people do that. Most of us don't begin saving until much later in life. A financial consultant will tell you how much you should save and where you should put it. If you wait until late in your working career, you can still save and have enough money for when you retire, but you're going to have to put a little more money into your 401(k) each week or month or whenever you fund your savings.

Keep in mind that rookie mistakes are correctable, but it's still best to avoid them. Why spend time and effort fixing problems that were unnecessary in the first place? In your early years, holding on to your money is always best. In your later years, make sure to consult professionals before investing in anything, especially a business start-up. Ultimately, making an amazing return on investment should not be the No. 1 financial goal—the preservation of your wealth should be.

GLOSSARY

Bonds: A debt security, similar to an IOU. When you purchase a bond, you are lending money to a government, municipality, or corporation.

Comparative Advantage: The ability of a person or a country to produce a particular good or service at a lower marginal and opportunity cost than another. Even if one country is more efficient in the production of all goods—has an absolute advantage—than the other, both countries will gain by trading with each other as long as they have different relative efficiencies.

Conservative: Disposed to preserve existing conditions, institutions, etc., or to restore traditional ones, and to limit change.

CPA: Certified Public Accountant (CPA) is the statutory title of qualified accountants in the United States who have passed the Uniform Certified Public Accountant Examination.

Enable: To make able; to give power, means, competence, or ability to; to authorize.

Entourage: A group of followers, especially of a person of high rank.

Financial Audit: The verification of the financial statements of a legal entity.

Financial Consultant: Also known as a financial adviser or financial planner, this is a professional who offers money management advice to individuals and businesses. Most people come to financial consultants looking for guidance on how to reach long-term financial goals, which may include a debt management plan, investment advice, and/or developing a savings plan. A business will sometimes hire a consultant for advice on managing money programs for its employees.

Liability: In financial accounting, a liability is defined as an obligation of an entity arising from past transactions or events, the settlement of which may result in the transfer or use of assets, provision of services, or other yielding of economic benefits in the future.

Municipal Funds: A mutual fund that invests in municipal bonds. These bond funds are popular among investors in high-income tax brackets.

Need: Something that is necessary for organisms to live a healthy life. Needs are distinguished from wants because the thwarting of needs causes a negative outcome, such as dysfunction or death. Needs can be objective and physical, such as the need for food, or they can be subjective and psychological, such as the need for self-esteem. On a social level, needs are sometimes controversial. Understanding needs and wants is important in the fields of politics, social science, and philosophy.

Pension: A regular and fixed payment made to a retired person as the result of his or her contributions to an organization's fund that has been set up for this purpose.

Portfolio: The securities held by an investor; the commercial paper held by a financial house (as a bank).

Power of Attorney: A legal instrument authorizing one to act as the attorney or agent of the grantor.

Prenuptial Agreement: A written contract between two people who are about to marry, setting out the terms of possession of assets, treatment of future earnings, control of the property of each, and potential division if the marriage is later dissolved. These agreements are fairly common if either or both parties have substantial assets, children from a prior marriage, potential inheritances, or high incomes, or if they've been "taken" by a prior spouse.

Residual Income: The amount of income that an individual has after all personal debts, including the mortgage, have been paid. This calculation is usually made on a monthly basis, after the monthly bills and debts are paid. Also, when a mortgage has been paid off in its entirety, the income that individual had been putting toward the mortgage becomes residual income.

Return on Investment (ROI): A performance measure used to evaluate the efficiency of an investment or to compare the efficiency of a number of different investments. To calculate ROI, the benefit (return) of an investment is divided by the cost of the investment; the result is expressed as a percentage or a ratio.

Stocks: In effect, part ownership of a company. When an individual buys a stock, he buys a stake in the assets and earnings of the company.

Poverty Mentality: A way of thinking that is said to perpetuate poverty because the focus is on what one doesn't have rather than what one does have.

Tax Rate: In a tax system and in economics, this describes the percentage at which a business or person is taxed.

Vested: Protected or established by law, commitment, tradition, ownership, etc.

Want: Something that is desired. It is said that every person has unlimited wants but limited resources. Thus, people cannot have everything they want and must look for the most affordable alternatives.

RESOURCES

BOOKS

Money Players, by Marc Isenberg

Financially Stupid People Are Everywhere: Don't Be One of Them, by Jason Kelly

Rich Dad, Poor Dad, by Robert Kiyosaki

The Money Book for the Young, Fabulous & Broke, by Suze Orman

The Total Money Makeover: A Proven Plan for Financial Fitness, by Dave Ramsey

Personal Finance for Dummies, by Eric Tyson

WEBSITES

Annual Credit Report—annualcreditreport.com

Provides a free copy of your credit report every twelve months from each credit-reporting company

E$Planner—basic.esplanner.com

Suggests how much to save, spend, and insure each year in order to meet your retirement goals

Internal Revenue Service—irs.gov

Answers tax questions and provides downloadable forms for filing

Learnvest—learnvest.com

Matches you with a real, live personal planner

Credit Karma—creditkarma.com
NOLO—nolo.com/legal-encyclopedia/personal-finance-retire
   ment
Provides free answers to personal finance questions as well as
   other legal and business inquiries

CONSULTATION SERVICES

Foyle Performance Coaching—focuses on the mental well-being
   of clients while helping them reach their full potential as pro-
   fessional or amateur athletes: FoylePerformanceCoaching.com
Foyle Consulting—provides strategic consulting for pro athletes:
   FoyleConsulting.com
National Basketball Retired Players Association—assists former
   players in their transition from the playing court into life after
   the game: LegendsofBasketball.com
National Basketball Players Association—nbpa.com
Assists current players in maximizing their opportunities and
   achieving their goals, both on and off the court
National Football League Players Association—nflplayers.com
Assures proper recognition and representation of players' interests
Major League Baseball Players Association—mlbpa.org
Protects and advances the interests of big-league players
Carla Lundblade's 10-point system
Carla Lundblade (www.carlalundblade.com) is a therapist special-
   izing in sports and celebrity culture. She came up with what she
   calls a "10-point system to help celebrities and professional ath-
   letes develop an awareness of the common issues encountered by
   athletes with a high-income and high-profile lifestyle."
The "Lundblade System" is as follows:

   1. Seek out professional investment specialists early on in
      your career.

2. Don't give in to showing off your new "richness" to teammates, fans, or loved ones. Remember: Up to 70 percent of them are going to be broke!

3. Never hire friends, family, or former coaches to manage your finances. Hire for expertise, not relationship.

4. Check the background of your financial advisers. Many have questionable pasts, or worse, criminal backgrounds directly related to money. Also, watch for people overcharging you for services.

5. Effectively handle and manage the flood of new people entering your life; don't let them handle you.

6. Limit paternity. Choose love relationships carefully and reduce the chance of having unplanned children. For some athletes, child support payments are their largest payouts.

7. Don't get married too young and don't think marrying your hometown sweetheart or someone who knew you before the success is always a smart decision. It's not.

8. Draw up a good prenuptial when you do get married. Not all prenuptials are created equal, so make sure yours is solid.

9. Don't get divorced. The divorce rate among professional athletes is 60 to 80 percent, and almost all happen in retirement. The athlete's peak earning periods are usually long over by this time, and making the same amount of money as he once did is virtually impossible.

10. Draw up a will. In steps 1 through 9 you've protected and nurtured the security of your bright financial future, so do the same for your family just in case you're not there to take care of them.

ACKNOWLEDGMENTS

Writing a book is an ambitious project for anyone, but for someone traveling nonstop all over the country for basketball games, the idea can be downright daunting. This book wouldn't have been possible without the help of many.

First, I want to thank Patrick Walsh, my financial consultant for the last twenty years, and Richard Cohen, my CPA. Rick's no-nonsense approach to taxes is just what I need to stay on the right financial path.

I'm also grateful for my stepfather, Jay Mandle, for always lending an ear to my concerns and for being the pain-in-the-butt third member of my financial team. And for my step-mother, Joan Mandle, the lady with the red-ink pen who takes no prisoners but always encourages as she pushes. Thank you for balancing mommyhood with rigorous academic pursuit.

A great thank-you to Shiyana Valentine, not only for encouraging me but for helping me edit my gibberish. Shiyana always believed I could write a book that would help people. Thank you for your continued belief in me and for pushing me to create my children's book series and to write for outlets like the *Orlando Sentinel*, my personal website, and *Athletes Quarterly* magazine.

A special thank-you to Chris Wilder for helping me to pull everything together in the end.

I also want to thank Lorisse Garcia and Joel Glass for sending me numerous articles on the subject of this book and for allowing me to complain to them unmercifully.

Special thanks to Irwin Soonachan for reading and re-reading this manuscript. His insight and advice have been immeasurable. Thank you for your hard work and dedication in helping bring this project to fruition.

I am indebted to Bobbie Dyer, division president of Dyer Mortgage Group, for her vast knowledge of finance, particularly in the areas of real estate, mortgages, and credit preservation.

Special praise goes out to Otis Smith, my former boss, for giving me the space to grow and for helping me follow my ambitions. Not many people balance work and family better than Otis does. Thanks for your support, brother.

Christopher Navalta, you rock. Thanks for interviewing several of my sources and helping me transcribe my stream of consciousness—all without judging me. Thanks for helping to edit my spelling and diction. You are indeed a friend.

I would like to thank Darrin Thurman for helping me with my research. Thanks also to my high-school English teacher, Nan Washburn, for taking a red pen to my book.

Thank you to Stephen Eriksen for his continued stewardship of my personal life, which freed me up to focus on this project.

I would like to thank Leland Thompson, executive coach and founder of Leland Thompson Consulting, for his unique insight and honesty in financial management.

Thanks to Derek Teasley and Kevin Cadogan for their brainstorming sessions and encouragement on this project.

And finally, thanks to the JFK University community and Alison Rhodius for supervising my master's thesis, out of which this book was born.

ABOUT THE AUTHOR

ADONAL FOYLE played thirteen seasons in the NBA: ten with the Golden State Warriors, three with the Orlando Magic, and one game with the Memphis Grizzlies. After hanging up his jersey, he served two seasons as the director of player development for the Orlando Magic.

Adonal graduated magna cum laude from Colgate University, with a degree in history. He earned his master's degree in sports psychology (which he began during his NBA career) from John F. Kennedy University in Pleasant Hill, California. His master's thesis, for which he interviewed numerous colleagues, was an in-depth study of the life changes experienced by NBA players upon retirement.

During his NBA career, Adonal served as first vice president of the National Basketball Players Association, representing NBA players during labor disputes and collective bargaining negotiations.

He is also the founder and president of two nonprofit organizations. His Kerosene Lamp Foundation empowers at-risk youths through athletics and academics camps, mentorship, and literacy initiatives. His other nonprofit, Democracy Matters, encourages young people to get involved in the political system and let their voices be heard.

Adonal has received numerous honors, including induction

into the World Sports Humanitarian Hall of Fame and the Co-SIDA Academic All-America Hall of Fame, and appointment as Goodwill Ambassador of St. Vincent and the Grenadines. He also received the NBA Players Association Community Contribution All-Star Award, and was named Social Change Agent (Greenlining Institute).

In his spare time, Adonal enjoys reading, wine-tasting, racquetball, traveling, and writing poetry.

CONTACT THE AUTHOR

www.AdonalFoyle.com
www.FoyleConsulting.com
Twitter.com/afoyle3131
Facebook.com/FoylesForum